THE FORBIDDEN ZONE

BY

MARY BORDEN

*

To the Poilus
who came that way in
1914-1918

WILLIAM HEINEMANN, LTD.,
London

Published 1929

CONTENTS

Part One
THE NORTH

Part Two
THE SOMME
Hospital Sketches

(continued)

CONTENTS

(*continued*)

POEMS

THE PREFACE

I have not invented anything in this book. The sketches and poems were written between 1914 and 1918, during four years of hospital work with the French Army. The five stories I have written recently from memory ; they recount true episodes that I cannot forget.

I have called the collection of fragments " The Forbidden Zone " because the strip of land immediately behind the zone of fire where I was stationed went by that name in the French Army. We were moved up and down inside it ; our hospital unit was shifted from Flanders to the Somme, then to Champagne, and then back again to Belgium, but we never left " La Zone Interdite."

To those who find these impressions confused, I would say that they are fragments of a great confusion. Any attempt to reduce them to order would require artifice on my part and would falsify them. To those on the other hand who find them unbearably plain, I would say that I have blurred the bare horror of facts and softened the reality in spite of myself, not because I wished to do so, but because I was incapable of a nearer approach to the truth.

I have dared to dedicate these pages to the Poilus who passed through our hands during the war, because I believe they would recognise the dimmed reality reflected in these pictures. But the book is not meant for them. They know, not only everything that is contained in it, but all the rest that can never be written.

The Author.

PART ONE

THE NORTH

BELGIUM

Mud : and a thin rain coming down to make more mud.

Mud : with scraps of iron lying in it and the straggling fragment of a nation, lolling, hanging about in the mud on the edge of disaster.

It is quiet here. The rain and the mud muffle the voice of the war that is growling beyond the horizon. But if you listen you can hear cataracts of iron pouring down channels in the sodden land, and you feel the earth trembling.

Back there is France, just behind the windmill. To the north, the coast ; a coast without a port, futile. On our right ? That's the road to Ypres. The less said about that road the better : no one goes down it for choice—it's British now. Ahead of us, then ? No, you can't get out that way. No, there's no frontier, just a bleeding edge, trenches. That's

where the enemy took his last bite, fastened
his iron teeth, and stuffed to bursting,
stopped devouring Belgium, left this strip,
these useless fields, these crumpled dwellings.

Cities ? None. Towns ? No whole ones.
Yes, there are half a dozen villages. But there
is plenty of mud, and a thin silent rain falling
to make more mud—mud with things lying in
it, wheels, broken motors, parts of houses,
graves.

This is what is left of Belgium. Come, I'll
show you. Here are trees drooping along a
canal, ploughed fields, roads leading into sand
dunes, roofless houses. There's a farm, an
old woman with a crooked back feeding chickens, a convoy of motor lorries round a barn ;
they squat like elephants. And here is a village
crouching in the mud : the cobblestone street
is slippery and smeared with refuse, and there
is a yellow cat sitting in a window. This is the
headquarters of the Belgian Army. You see
those men, lolling in the doorways—uncouth,
dishevelled, dirty ? They are soldiers. You
can read on their heavy jowls, in their stupi-
fied, patient, hopeless eyes, how boring it is to
be a hero.

2

The king is here. His office is in the school-room down the street, a little way past the church, just beyond the dung heap. If we wait we may see him. Let's stand with these people in the rain and wait.

A band is going to play to the army. Yes, I told you, this is the army—these stolid men standing aimlessly in the drizzle, and these who come stumbling along the slippery ditches, and those leaning in degraded door-ways. They fought their way out of Liege and Namur, followed the king here ; they are what is left of plucky little Belgium's heroic army.

And the song of the nation that comes from the horns in the front of the wine shop, the song that sounds like the bleating of sheep, can it help them ? Can it deceive them ? Can it whisk from their faces the stale despair, the unutterable boredom, and brighten their disappointed eyes ? They are so few, and they have nothing to do but stand in the rain wait-ing. When the band stops they will disappear into the estaminet to warm their stomachs with wine and cuddle the round-cheeked girls. What else can they do ? The French are on one side of them, the British on the other, and the enemy in front. They cannot go back ; to go back is to retreat, and they have been retreating ever since they can remember. They can retreat no farther. This village is where they stop. At one end of it is a pigsty, at the other end is a grave-yard, and all about are flats of mud. Can the noise, the rhythmical beating of the drum, the piping, the hoarse shrieking, help these men, make them believe, make them glad to be heroes? They have nowhere to go now and nothing to do. There is nothing but mud all about, and a soft fine rain coming down to make more mud—mud with a broken fragment of a nation lolling in it, hanging about waiting in it behind the shelter of a disaster that has been accomplished.

Come away, for God's sake—come away. Let's go back to Dunkerque. The king? Didn't you see him ? He came out of the school-house some time ago and drove away toward the sand-dunes—a big fair man in uniform. You didn't notice ? Never mind. Come away.

4

BOMBARDMENT

THE wide sweet heaven was filling with light: the perfect dome of night was changing into day. A million silver worlds dissolved from above the earth : the sun was about to rise in stillness : no wind stirred.

A speck appeared in the great immensity. It was an aeroplane travelling high through the mysterious twilight. The sound of the whirring of its engine was lost in the depthless air : like a ghost it flew through the impalpable firmament : it was the only thing that moved in heaven and earth.

The unconscious map lay spread out beneath it : the wide plain, the long white beach and the sea, lay there exposed to its speeding eye.

On the face of the plain were villages and cities ; the dwellings of men who had put their trust in the heavens and had dared to people the earth.

The aeroplane turned in the sky and began circling over the town.

The town far below was asleep. It lay pillowed on the secure shore ; violet shadows leaned against its pale buildings ; there was no movement in its streets ; no smoke from its chimneys. The ships lay still in the deep close harbour ; their masts rose out of the green water like reeds thickly growing with the great funnels and turrets of warships like strange plants among them. The sea beyond the strong breakwater was smooth as a silver plate ; there was no sound anywhere.

The aeroplane descended in slow spirals upon the town, tracing an invisible path through the pearly air. It was as if a messenger from heaven were descending upon the people of the town who dreamed.

Suddenly a scream burst from the throat of the church tower. For an instant the sky seemed to shiver with the stab of that wail of terror rising from the great stone throat. Surely the town would waken in a panic— and yet, no, nothing stirred. There was no sound or movement in any street and the sky gave back no sign.

The aeroplane continued to descend until it looked from the church tower like a mosquito ; then there dropped something from it that flashed through the air, a spark of fire.

Silence had followed the scream.

The aeroplane, superbly poised now in the spotless sky, watched the buildings below it as if waiting for some strange thing to happen ; and presently, as if exorcised by the magic eye of that insect, a cluster of houses collapsed, while a roar burst from the wounded earth.

The bombardment had commenced. The big gun hiding in the sand-dunes in Belgium had obeyed the signal.

Still, the neat surface of the wide city showed no change, save in that one spot where the houses had fallen. How slow to wake the town was ! The daylight brightened, painting the surfaces of the buildings with pale rose and primrose. The clean empty streets cut the city into firm blocks of buildings ; the pattern of the town spread out on the earth, with its neat edges marked by walls and canals, gleamed like a varnished map.

Then the siren in the church tower

screamed again; its wail was followed by a second roar and a ragged hole yawned in the open square in the middle of the town.

The aeroplane circled smoothly, watching.

And at last signs of terror and bewilderment appeared in the human ant hill beneath it. Distracted midgets swarmed from the houses : this way and that they scurried, diving into openings in the ground : swift armoured beetles rushed through the streets ; white jets of steam rose from the locomotives in the station yard : the harbour throbbed.

Again there was a great noise, and a cloud of debris was flung into the air as from a volcano, and flames leapt after it. A part of the wharf with a shed on it reeled drunkenly into the sea with a splash.

The white beach was crawling now with vermin ; the human hive swarmed out on to the sands. Their eyes were fixed on the evil flying thing in the sky and at each explosion they fell on their faces like frantic worshippers.

The aeroplane cavorted, whirling after its tail in an ecstacy of self-gratification. Down among the sand-dunes it could see the tiny

8

black figures of men at the anti-aircraft guns. These were the defenders of the town ; they had orders to shoot to death a mosquito floating in boundless heaven. The little clouds that burst in the sunlight were like materialised kisses.

The face of the city had begun to show a curious change. Scars appeared on it like the marks of smallpox and as these thickened on its trim surface, it seemed as if it were being attacked by an invisible and gigantic beast, who was tearing and gnawing it with claws and teeth. Gashes appeared in its streets, long wounds with ragged edges. Helpless, spread . out to the heavens, it grimaced with mutilated features.

Nevertheless the sun rose, touching the aeroplane with gold, and the aeroplane laughed. It laughed at the convulsed face of the town, at the beach crawling with vermin, at the ant people swarming through the gates of the city along the white roads ; it laughed at the warships moving out of the harbour one by one in stately procession, the mouths of their guns gaping helplessly in their armoured sides. With a last flick of its glittering wings, it darted downward defiant, dodging the kisses of shrapnel, luring them, teasing them, playing with them : then, its message delivered, its sport over, it flew up and away in the sunshine and disappeared. A speck in the infinite sky, then nothing—and the town was left in convulsions.

THE CAPTIVE BALLOON

THERE is a captive balloon in the sky, just over there. It looks like an oyster floating in the sky.

They say that a man lives in the balloon. They say that from the balloon you can see the enemy's trenches and the country behind that is held by the enemy, but from here we can see nothing, only trees and farmhouses and carts going along the road, and the captive balloon.

Aeroplanes sail over our heads sometimes. They gleam in the sun, they move past with a great whirring, they fly fearlessly toward the enemy's country. They whirl about and disappear and come again, swooping down over us with arrogant wings. They are beautiful, proud and adventurous.

But the captive balloon is tied forever by a string to a cabbage field. It has been just over there ever since we have been here and that is a long time now. It never moves. It never comes down or goes up. It floats there while the biplanes and the monoplanes circle round it.

What does it do? It is an oyster in the sky, keeping an eye on the Germans.

THE SQUARE

BELOW my window in the big bright square a struggle is going on between the machines of war and the people of the town. There are the motor cars of the army, the limousines, and the touring cars and the motor lorries and the ambulances ; and there are the little bare-headed women of the town with baskets on their arms who try to push the monsters out of their way.

The motors come in and go out of the four corners of the square, and they stand panting and snorting in the middle of it. The limousines are full of smart men in uniforms with silver hair and gold braid on their round red hats. The touring cars, too, are full of uniforms, but on the faces of the young men who drive them is a look of exhaustion and excitement. The motors make a great noise and a great smell and a great dust. They come into

13

the square, hooting and shrieking ; they draw up in the square with grinding brakes. The men in them get out with a flourish of capes : they stamp on the pavement with heavy boots; they salute one another stiffly like wooden toys, then disappear into the buildings where they hold murderous conferences and make elaborate plans of massacre.

The motor cars have all gone wrong. They are queer. They are not doing what they were designed to do when they were turned out of the factories. The limousines were made to carry ladies to places of amusement: they are carrying generals to places of killing. The limousines and the touring cars and the motor lorries are all debauched; they have a depraved look; their springs sag, their wheels waver; their bodies lean to one side. The elegant limousines that carry the generals are crusted with old mud; the leather cushions of the touring cars are in tatters; the great motor lorries crouch under vast burdens. They crouch in the square ashamed, deformed, very weary; their unspeakable burdens bulge under canvas coverings. Only the snobbish ambulances with the red crosses on their sides have self-assurance. They have the self-assurance of amateurs.

The business of killing and the business of living go on together in the square beneath the many windows, jostling each other.

The little women of the town are busy; they are dressed in black; they have children with them. Some lead children by the hand, others are big with children yet unborn. But all the women are busy. They ignore the motors; they do not see the fine scowling generals, nor the strained excited faces in the fast touring cars, nor the provisions of war under their lumpy coverings. They do not even wonder what is in the ambulances. They are too busy. They scurry across to the shops, instinctively dodging, and come out again with bundles; they talk to each other a little without smiling; they stare in front of them; they are staring at life; they are thinking about the business of living.

On Saturdays they put up their booths on the cobble stones and hold their market. The motors have to go round another way on market days. There is no room in the square for the generals, nor for the dying men in the ambulances. The women are there. They buy and sell their saucepans and their linen and their spools of thread and their fowls and their flowers; they bargain and they chatter; they provide for their houses and their children; they give oranges to their children, and put away their coppers in their deep pockets.

As for the men on the stretchers inside the smart ambulances with the bright red crosses, they do not know about the women in the square. They cannot hear their chattering, nor see the children sucking oranges; they can see nothing and hear nothing of the life that is going on in the square; they are lying on their backs in the dark canvas bellies of the ambulances, staring at death. They do not know that on Saturday mornings their road does not lie through the big bright square because the little women of the town are busy with their market.

SENTINELS

ALL these little men coming out of their boxes along the road—.

The boxes are oblong. They stand on end by the ragged ditches. The men pop out of the boxes into the middle of the road. They are blurred and shapeless. They wave dirty flags in weary warning. A motor car slows up and stops before the box. The languid menace of these figures stops it; their joyless power holds it with its engines panting.

The coats of the little men who come out of the boxes are too big for them; their rifles with the bayonets are too heavy. The light of the sky in the daytime is too strong, and the darkness of the night is too dark, and the many motors that pass the barriers are too many. The vague vast meaning of their minute task is too much for them.

It is stupid to live in an oblong box in a

ditch, and to pop out at the sound of a motor and wave a flag and look at a piece of blue paper or a piece of pink paper with writing on it that is hard to read. There is a name written on the paper, but how is one to know whether the name written on the paper is the name that was given to the man in the motor by his parents when he was a baby in a cradle? How is one to know? It is one's business to look at the paper and at the man's face. What good does that do? What does it matter? It is one's duty to look at the paper. It is one's duty to look at the man. It is one's duty to find out where he has come from and where he is going. La Panne, Dunkerque, Bourburg, Calais, Boulogne; Boulogne, Calais, Bourburg, Dunkerque, La Panne, it is always the same. It is always written there on the paper, with the stamp and the signature of some well-educated officer who sits in some warm room before piles of papers. These papers wander out from his room along the road.

It is always the same on the road. It is always the same. All these motor cars full of men keep coming along the road—the long road that leads to the war. Sometimes it is hot and there is sunlight and dust on the road, and the smell of petrol is strong; sometimes it is cold and the rain beats down from the sky; sometimes it is night and there is a lantern to wave instead of a flag, and there is the fear of falling asleep. But the road is always the same and the box by the road is always the same, and deep down there is the same truth always.

All these motors and all these scornful men that stop to show impatient papers will disappear up the road for ever. Even those who come down the road will go up again and will be destroyed and will never come back. So it is good to be in the box. As long as one is in the box one will not be destroyed. These fools who are angry because they are stopped on the road that leads to the war, they will be destroyed. The generals who do not look and the colonels who glance sideways, and the lieutenants who make bad jokes—the English and the French and the Belgians—they will all be destroyed.

They wear fine uniforms. Their faces are clean. They have been eating good food. They receive back their papers disdainfully. They wear gloves. They will be destroyed with their gold braid and their medals and the good food inside them.

Their motors dash off flinging mud into the face from their hind wheels. They disappear. The road is empty.

THERE was no sign of horror in the heavens or upon the earth The summer world was deep, immense, beautiful. High white clouds were moving slowly towards Belgium, moving without movement through a sky ineffably blue, superb castles of white vapour, floating towards a land called No Man's Land, and their shadows were flung like banners far below over the green meadows and fields of yellow corn.

An aeroplane was visiting the romantic city of the sky. A fearless, capricious, gay glittering creature of pleasure, it flew through the glistening portals and disappeared, bent on mysterious adventure.

The smiling country was enjoying itself. The caress of the wind sent shudders of pleasure through the corn and a fluttering delight through the trees. Along the road banks scarlet poppies were winking their little black eyes. Like grizzled dwarfs squatting on pedestals in the fields, the windmills waved their arms in grotesque gaiety.

War had that day the aspect of a country fair. The armies were gipsy caravans vagabonding over the country. Swarms of little men were housekeeping in the open. Their camp fires, their pots and pans, and their garments hung out to dry on bushes, twinkled and fluttered through the furbelowed country side. Here and there near a stream, a cluster of tents, gaudily painted, suggested a circus.

The snug villages tucked between the fields of high golden corn and scattered clumps of woodland hummed like beehives, sheltering an army in their warm farmyards and barns and cottages, and the army in reserve waited comfortably, sharing the lovely day with the cattle, the great farm horses, the pigs and chickens.

Ten miles from the Belgian frontier a low-browed, moody town dozed on the banks of a canal. Folded close between its great gates, it was deep as a dark well in the midst of the bright flighty country. The dull ochre walls of the houses soaked up the sunlight. Their shutters were closed. The barges in the canal were motionless, their great bosoms sunk deep in the cool water. From the quiet streets and close-lidded houses the spirit of the place was being distilled in the sunlight. It was as if the sun were drawing the melancholy soul out of the weary, proud old body of the town. Reluctantly it gave up its secret. The memories of its troubled history and of how it had defended a passionate egoism on the threshold of an alien nation, spread upon the sunny air like a dark and bitter perfume.

A regiment was marching along the high road towards the town. In the distance, looking towards Belgium, you could see it coming down the white road. It was a shadow moving across the bright surface of the country against the wind and against the shadows of the clouds. It looked like the shadow of a snake.

There was, however, no snake visible in the lovely sky, and on a nearer view the shadow became a column of hunchbacks, a herd of deformed creatures driven on together, each one like another one.

It was a French territorial regiment. It had come out of the trenches that morning, and from the trenches it was marching toward the town.

It was a moving mass of men covered over with the cloth of fatigue. Over them was their suffocating weariness, and under them was the dust of the road. They moved along, bending forward as if the space between the weight that lay on them and the dusty road under them was not wide enough to hold them upright. They moved laboriously through the dust, as if they were dragging chains. But there was no sound from them save the dull sound of their feet tramping the road.

The regiment was a regiment of old men. Their faces were old and their clothes were old and their bodies were old, and the spirit in them was old. There was no youth in any one of them.

They marched steadily along the road. Their gait was the steady jolting gait of weary animals. They did not look quite like men. One could not be certain what kind of men they were. One could only be certain that they were not young. They had not quite the colour nor the shape of men. The war had spread over them its own colour. They were dark against the bright mirage of summer. They were of a deep, dull courageous hue. Their faces and their hands and their coats were all stained with the same stain, no longer blue, no longer brown. Fatigue and suffering and dirt had soaked through them and had made them this colour.

And they were all deformed, and certainly their deformity was the deformity of the war. They were not misshapen in different ways. They were all misshapen in the same way. Each one was deformed like the next one. Each one had been twisted and bent in the same way. Each one carried the same burden that bowed his back, the same knapsack, the same roll of blanket, the same flask, the same dangling box, the same gun. Each one dragged swollen feet in the same thick-crusted boots. The same machine had twisted and bent them all. They did not look quite like men, and yet they were men.

Nor did they behave like men. They did not look about them as they marched along the road. They did not talk as they marched close together. They did not stop marching, never for a moment did they stop marching. They did not shift their burdens to ease them. They did not notice the milestones as they passed. They paid no attention to the signposts at the cross roads. They did not wipe the sweat off their faces. They did not behave like men walking through pleasant country, and yet they assuredly were men.

I saw in their eyes that they were men. They marched with their eyes fixed on the rough bent backs of those in front, on the rough backs of their companions who were too old to be comrades. And in their deep fixed eyes, sunk under grizzled eyebrows, there was a strange expression, the expression of profound knowledge. They were old men and they knew. There were many things they did not know; they did not know where they were going; they did not know why they were going there; they did not know how far they had to go, or how long they would rest there; but two things they did know; they knew that they were not going home, and they knew that they were condemned to death. They

26

knew this; they had always known. They understood and they did not complain. France was at war. They were old men. Their sons had been killed. They were taking the place of their sons.

There was no elasticity in them, nor any enthusiasm, nor any passion; but they were patient. Being old men, there was nothing they could not accept; there was nothing they could not endure. They had endured fatigue and cold and hunger and wet. They had endured so long that they had ceased to think about these things. Their weariness was a thing of such long standing that they thought of it no more. Their uncleanness had become a habit to them. Suffering was a part of their rations. They were acclimatised to misery. Death was a part of the equipment they carried always with them. The war had no interest for them nor any terror. They accepted the war. It was a thing to be endured. They were enduring it.

There was only one thing they wanted, and this thing they wanted without hope. They wanted to go home, and they knew they were not going home.

Out of the deep comfort of the warm dear holes they had dug for themselves in the land they loved, these old men had been called to war, the bleak desert of death. Each one had been torn up out of the deep place he had made. Like old trees, strong rooted, they had grown into the soil of France, and they had been torn up and carted away to die, and in the place each one had left there was a gaping hole.

They remembered their homes as they marched along the road. They did not look about them as they walked through the bright country that was enjoying itself, because this country was not their home and they were too tired to look up.

They were coming away from the trenches and they were tired. They were relieved of the strain of imminent death, but the relief made them only more tired. And what was the good of coming away from the trenches if they were not going home? Long ago they had gone into the trenches. They had crawled laboriously into them, their old bodies creaking, their gouty souls wincing, and they had learned how to live in those ditches.

Carefully with great caution they had learned how to endure them. They had smoked innumerable pipes in them and had chewed loaves of bread; they had slept and waked and received letters from home. Then, with the same creaking of their joints they had come out of the trenches. Some of them had not come out, but those that were left had come out.

Now they were going along the road.

They did not know where they were going; they only knew that they were not going home. It was all the same to them as long as they could not go home.

The aeroplane, glittering in the sun, was still circling through the citadel of the sky. High it flew. It flew high ! It flew higher again, and still higher.

The regiment was chained to the earth. The men were chained to the ground. They were heavy; they were fastened down. The mass of them jolted along, a dark weight scraping the road. Their flag alone was lifted. It moved fluttering above their heads, tattered and soiled. It was there for an emblem of hope. They ignored it. They did not see it.

Long ago they had ceased to regard it.

So they marched toward the town.

In the centre of the big sleepy square of the town was a group of fine little men in costume. They were waiting for the regiment that was marching along the road, and they were waiting for the General who commanded the army, the General-in-Chief, their own General. These fine little men were officers. One could not be certain that they had anything to do with the war, but one could be certain that they were officers. Their trim figures, polished and clean and neatly put together and nicely covered in scarlet and blue cloth and brown leather, stood upright in the centre of the square. The wide expanse of cobblestones on which they stood glistened like a sheet of opaque glass. From the four sides of the square the wise houses watched under ruminating brows. It was difficult to tell what the houses thought of the officers in the square. It was difficult to tell what the officers were doing there in the middle of the square. Certainly they were waiting, but they seemed to be busily, nervously waiting. They could not keep still. They seemed conscious of the

30

stare of the houses. They drew themselves up
very straight. Their arms made quick gestures; their gloved hands twirled their mous-
taches; their neat heels tapped the pavement
smartly. They bowed to one another elaborately.

There was variety among these officers. No
one was like another one. Not one had gestures like another one. Not one had clothes
like another one. Certainly they were indi-
viduals. One was a slim, graceful one; one
was a flabby one; one was an elegant one; one
a tall, very stiff one; one was a pot-bellied one.
Each remained the same one he had been before the war. They were varnished over with
a military varnish, but beneath the varnish
appeared distinctly the small individuality of
each one. It was curious to see such fine
shiny men in the centre of the old haggard
town.

The hard knobbled palm of the square held
them up to the view of the sky.

Through the east gate of the town the regiment came into the town dragging its weight
and its darkness, and it poured its darkness
into the square. It poured through the gap of

the street into the square, and it came to a
stand. It was a dark mass of tenacity, inert,
incurious, obstinate, one man beside another
man, each one like the next one, close packed
together between the pale dreaming houses.

The regiment brought truth into the
square. It was a fact, a darkness, a weight
filling one side of the square.

And with the regiment war appeared in the
square.

The town shuddered under the tramping
feet of the regiment.

The men of the regiment stood close packed
together. The mass of their round metal
helmets gleamed like a beach of smooth pebbles
before the windows of the houses, and their
bayonets shot up like a forest of knives flashing
in the sunlight.

The town shuddered. But there was sympathy between the regiment and the town.

The town said to the regiment:

" You old ones, you are strangers; but we
know you. You come from the war. You are
welcome."

The regiment said to the town:

" You are kind, but you'd do well to keep

your welcome for those who can use it. We are old. We want nothing since we cannot go home."

" Rest here awhile, old ones," repeated the town.

" No, we cannot stay. We do not belong here. You are old, too, like us; but we are too tired to make friends with you, though we thank you."

The group of officers said to the regiment:

" Look spry now. You're to be inspected by the General, and we are to receive decorations."

The regiment didn't answer. It had nothing to say to the staff officers. It did not recognise them. Its own officers—yes; but these it did not know, and the staff officers were embarrassed by the obstinacy and the stupidity and weariness of the regiment. They fidgeted on the edge of its darkness.

While the regiment and the officers waited in the square for the General, the aeroplane flew down from the cloud castles in the sky and circled over the town crying gaily:

"Look at me. Look at me, you heavy old ones, I can fly."

The officers looked up at the aeroplane. The regiment did not look up.

The officers said to themselves:

"That silly aeroplane is amusing itself, but we are going to receive decorations."

The regiment remained silent. It took no notice.

A bugle sounded, heralding the approach of the General, but instead of the General a woman came into the square. She came in a motor with glass windows. Her shining car stopped in front of the regiment. She opened the door of the motor and put out her white foot and stepped down, and her delicate body dressed in the white uniform of a hospital was exposed to the view of the officers and the regiment. Her head was bound close with a white kerchief. A red cross burned on her forehead.

She was a beautiful animal dressed as a nun and branded with a red cross. Her shadowy eyes said to the regiment:

"I came to the war to nurse you and comfort you."

The regiment said nothing. It did not know what to say. It was merely puzzled.

34

Her red mouth said to the officers:

"I am here for you."

And the officers said:

"We know why you are here."

The eyes of the officers followed the white shining woman as she moved through the sunlight, and they rested on her as she stood in a shadowed doorway.

The presence of the woman was a teasing current of delight touching the officers.

To the regiment the woman was a puzzle, but the old ones were too tired to bother about puzzles.

To the town she was a strange fantastic thing, like a white peacock.

The town said to itself: "This curious creature has gone astray. It has the appearance of being expensive. It must have escaped from its owner who, no doubt, prizes it highly; but that is none of our business."

The clock in the church tower marked three o'clock.

Suddenly a cry burst from the regiment, and a shout burst from the trumpets and horns and drums of the regiment. It rang through the square shivering against the houses. The

35

little people of the town came to their doorways. The rosy faces of the comfortable women and the round children spread round the square like a smile, and the hoarse passionate voice of the old rusty regiment rose bravely in welcome.

The General came.

He appeared at the far end of the square, a small solid figure standing alone. He existed apart, isolated. He stood at a distance, a solitary man, concentrating the attention of the town.

He came across the square alone, growing larger and larger as he came. He covered the ground with long strides. His gloved hand was on the hilt of his sword. When he reached the centre of the square, he wheeled and faced the regiment, a stone giant, solid as granite, commanding the attention of every man in the square. He ignored the officers and faced the regiment. And the town watching saw a curious thing. The bodies of the hunchbacks straightened under the eyes of the General. It was as if the iron arm of the stone man raised to salute them had lifted the weariness from the deformed shoulders of those old ones.

36

It was evident to the town that the General understood the regiment. It was evident that he knew what they knew. And with this dark knowledge he faced them. The trumpets and drums were hushed. A strange silence filled the square, and in silence the General summoned the regiment to meet his eyes. He took full in the face its dumb message. The weight he had lifted from it fell on him. The darkness drowning it flowed into him. He accepted it. He did not dodge it or bend under the weight of it. He stood rigid before the eyes of the regiment challenging its knowledge. The weary eyes of the old territorials were fixed on his white head and deep stony face. They searched him, and they saw that he knew what they knew, that there was nothing about the war that he didn't know, and they were satisfied.

The General said to the regiment:

"You are mine. Your sons have been killed. France had need of you and you came. You must die for France as your sons died. You left your homes to come to the war. You will never go home again. You will go back to the trenches. It is I who will send you back there.

37

Again and again you will go back to those ditches, by my orders, until you are killed as your sons were killed. You are mine for the war. I carry the weight of your obedience and your patience. You will be patient until death. I know you."

The regiment answered the General:

"It is for our homes and for our sons. We are here because our sons are gone to protect the homes we cannot go back to. You are the one we obey."

There was truth between the regiment and the General.

And the old town looking on, said:

"Clearly this is a great man. A hundred years ago there came here such a one as this, and he was a great man. We, too, are acquainted with war and with armies. We have seen thousands of little men, and we have seen some big men. We know that this is a great man."

From the regiment the General turned to the officers and the town perceived that the relation of the General to his officers was a complex thing. It was as complicated as a formal dance or pantomime on a stage. The officers knew their steps. They had apparently rehearsed the performance. The General treated the officers with elaborate ceremony. He was there to decorate them. The decorating of the officers was a ceremony, and he performed the ceremony with the skill of an actor. It was a pretty play in which the General played the principal rôle. He played it with solemnity. He saluted each one in turn, the long one, and the pale one and the pot-bellied one. He drew his sword from its scabbard; it flashed in the sun as he laid it upon their shoulders. On the left shoulder and upon the right shoulder of the Colonel he laid his sword. He pinned a medal on the Colonel's elegant chest and then he kissed him on the left cheek and on the right cheek. He did the same with each officer in turn. He called each one by name and addressed him in a loud voice of commendation. He laid on each one his sword and he kissed each one on both cheeks, and on the chest of each one he left a bit of ribbon and a bright medal.

The regiment in the background was the chorus for this pretty play. After each kiss and each decoration the trumpets and drums of the regiment cried aloud in congratulation.

Kisses and bits of ribbon and a graceful flashing sword, these little things passed between the General and his officers. No truth passed between them—nothing but a play.

And the play was ended.

And the General went away as he had come, taking with him the pride and the courage that he had brought into the square.

The face of the town grew dull as it watched him go. The women and the children disappeared into the dim houses. The white strange woman looked after him with vague, troubled eyes, not noticing the officers who advanced towards her, elaborately bowing.

The regiment lowered its bayonets at his going and bowed its shoulders. Its darkness grew more dark, and its weariness more heavy. When the General had gone it became again a shapeless mass of dark, weary hunchbacks.

The clock in the church tower marked five o'clock when the regiment left the square. It marched out of the town and along the road as it had come.

A regiment of old men.

They did not know where they were going. It did not matter to them where they were going. They did not look about them as they marched. They did not look before them, nor behind them. They did not look up at the cloudless sky, nor did they wonder where the clouds had gone. They did not remember the beautiful clouds of the morning that had sailed serenely over the enemy's country. They did not remember the sympathy of the town, nor the complacency of that fine little group of officers, nor the glittering of the bright medals, nor the insolence of the white woman who watched. They did not very much remember the grandeur of the General, nor the pride they had known in the General. They remembered their homes. The sweat ran down their faces under their helmets. Their feet were heavy on the road. They marched steadily, jolting along, patient, weary animals who remembered.

There was no sign of horror upon the earth. There was not a cloud in the sky. The afternoon sunlight was golden over the land. The regiment passed like a shadow through the bright country and was lost to view.

THE beach was long and smooth and the colour of cream. The woman sitting in the sun stroked the beach with the pink palm of her hand and said to herself, "The beach is perfect, the sun is perfect, the sea is perfect. How pretty the little waves are, curling up the beach. They are perfectly lovely. They are like a lace frill to the beach. And the sea is a perfectly heavenly blue. It is odd to think of how old the beach is and how old the sea is, and how much older that old, old fellow, the fiery sun. The face of the beach is smooth as cream and the sea to-day is a smiling infant, twinkling and dimpling, and the sun is delicious; it is burning hot, like youth itself. It is good to be alive. It is good to be young." But she could not say this aloud so she said to the man beside her in the wheel chair:

"How many millions of years has it taken to

make the beach? How many snails have left their shells behind them, do you think, to make all this fine powdery sand? A million billion?" She let the sand run through her strong white fingers and smiled, blinking in the sun and looked away from the man in the invalid chair beside her toward the horizon.

The man wriggled and hitched himself clumsily up in his chair; an ugly grimace pulled his pale face to one side. He dared not look down over the arm of his wheel chair at the bright head of the woman sitting beside him. Her hair burned in the sunlight; her cheeks were pink. He stole a timid, furtive look. Yes, she was as beautiful as a child. She was perfectly lovely. A groan escaped him, or was it only a sigh?

She looked up quickly. "What is it, darling? Are you in pain? Are you tired? Shall we go back?" Her voice sounded in the immense quiet of the beach like a cricket chirping, but the word "darling" went on sounding and sounding like a little hollow bell while she searched his features, trying to find his old face, the one she knew, trying to work a magic on him, remove and replace the sunken eyes, the pinched nose, the bloodless wry mouth. "He's not a stranger," she said to herself. "He's not." And she heard the faint mocking echo, "Darling, darling," ringing far away as if a bell-buoy out on the water were saying "Darling, darling," to make the little waves laugh.

"It's only my foot, my left foot. Funny, isn't it, that it goes on throbbing. They cut it off two months ago." He jerked a hand backward. "It's damn queer when you think of it. The old foot begins the old game, then I look down and it's not there any more, and I'm fooled again." He laughed. His laughter was such a tiny sound in the great murmur of the morning that it might have been a sand-fly laughing. He was thinking, "What will become of us? She is young and healthy. She is as beautiful as a child. What shall we do about it?" And looking into her eyes he saw the same question, "What shall we do?" and looked quickly away again. So did she.

She looked past him at the row of ugly villas above the beach. Narrow houses, each like a chimney, tightly wedged together, wedges of cheap brick and plaster with battered wooden balconies. They were new and shabby and derelict. All had their shutters up. All the doors were bolted. How stuffy it must be in those deserted villas, in all those abandoned bedrooms and kitchens and parlours. Probably there were sand-shoes and bathing dresses and old towels and saucepans and blankets rotting inside them with the sand drifting in. Probably the window panes behind the shutters were broken and the mirrors cracked. Perhaps when the aeroplanes dropped bombs on the town, pictures fell down and mirrors and the china in the dark china closets cracked inside these pleasure houses. Who had built them?

"Cowards built them," he said in his new bitter, rasping voice, the voice of a peevish, irritable sandfly. "Built them to make love in, to cuddle in, to sleep in, hide in. Now they're empty. The blighters have left them to rot there. Rotten, I call it, leaving the swanky plage to go to the bad like that, just because there's a war on. A little jazz now and a baccarat table would make all the difference, wouldn't it? It would cheer us up. You'd dance and I'd have a go at the tables. That's

the casino over there, that big thing; that's not
empty, that's crowded, but I don't advise you
to go there. I don't think you'd like it. It's
not your kind of a crowd. It's all right for me,
but not for you. No, it wouldn't do for you—
not even on a gala night.

"They've a gala night in our casino when-
ever there's a battle. Funny sort of place.
You should watch the motors drive up then.
The rush begins about ten in the evening and
goes on till morning. Quite like Deauville
the night of the Grand Prix. You never saw
such a crowd. They all rush there from the
front, you know—the way they do from the
race-course—though, to be sure, it is not
quite the real thing—not a really smart crowd.
No, not precisely, though the wasters in
Deauville weren't much to look at, were they?
Still, our crowd here aren't precisely wasters.
Gamblers, of course, down and outs, wrecks
—all gone to pieces, parts of 'em missing, you
know, tops of their heads gone, or one of their
legs. When they take their places at the
tables, the croupiers—that is to say, the doctors—look them over. Come closer, I'll
whisper it. Some of them have no faces."

46

"Darling, don't." She covered her own face, closed her ears to his tiny voice and listened desperately with all her minute will to the large tranquil murmur of the sea. "Darling, darling," far out the bell-buoy was sounding.

"Bless you," said the thin, sharp, exasperated sandfly voice beside her. "Little things like that don't keep us away. If we can't walk in we get carried in. All that's needed is a ticket. It's tied to you like a luggage label. It has your name on it in case you don't remember your name. You needn't have a face, but a ticket you must have to get into our casino."

"Stop, darling—darling, stop!"

"It's a funny place. There's a skating rink. You ought to see it. You go through the baccarat rooms and the dance hall to get to it. They're all full of beds. Rows of beds under the big crystal chandeliers, rows of beds under the big gilt mirrors, and the skating rink is full of beds, too. The sun blazes down through the glass roof. It's like a hot-house in Kew Gardens. There's that dank smell of a rotting swamp, the smell of gas gangrene.

47

Men with gas gangrene turn green, you know, like rotting plants." He laughed. Then he was silent. He looked at her cowering in the sand, her hands covering her face, and looked away again.

He wondered why he had told her these things. He loved her. He hated her. He was afraid of her. He did not want her to be kind to him. He could never touch her again and he was tied to her. He was rotting and he was tied to her perfection. He had no power over her any more but the power of infecting her with his corruption. He could never make her happy. He could only make her suffer. His one luxury now was jealousy of her perfection, and his one delight would be to give in to the temptation to make her suffer. He could only reach her that way. It would be his revenge on the war.

He was not aware of these thoughts. He was too busy with other little false thoughts. He was saying to himself, "I will let her go. I will send her away. Once we are at home again, I will say good-bye to her." But he knew that he was incapable of letting her go.

He closed his eyes. He said to himself

48

"The smell of the sea is good, but the odour that oozes from the windows of the casino is bad. I can smell it from here. I can't get the smell of it out of my nose. It is my own smell," and his wasted greenish face twitched in disgust.

She looked at him. "I love him," she said to herself. "I love him," she repeated. "But can I go on loving him?" She whispered, "Can I? I must." She said, "I must love him, now more than ever, but where is he?"

She looked round her as if to find the man he once had been. There were other women on the beach, women in black and old men and children with buckets and spades, people of the town. They seemed to be glad to be alive. No one seemed to be thinking of the war.

The beach was long and smooth and the colour of cream. The beach was perfect; the sun perfectly delicious; the sea was perfectly calm. The man in the wheel chair and the woman beside him were no bigger than flies on the sand. The women and children and old men were specks.

Far out on the sea there was an object;

there were two objects. The people on the beach could scarcely distinguish them. They peered through the sunshine while the children rolled in the sand, and they heard the sound of a distant hammer tapping.

"They are firing out at sea," said someone to someone.

How perfect the beach is. The sea is a perfectly heavenly blue. Behind the windows of the casino, under the great crystal chandeliers, men lie in narrow beds. They lie in queer postures with their greenish faces turned up. Their white bandages are reflected in the sombre gilt mirrors. There is no sound anywhere but the murmur of the sea and the whispering of the waves on the sand, and the tap tap of a hammer coming from a great distance across the water, and the bell-buoy that seems to say, "Darling, darling."

MOONLIGHT

THE moonlight is a pool of silver on the lino-
leum floor. It glints on the enamel wash-
basin and slop pail. I can almost see the moon
reflected in the slop pail. Everything in my
cubicle is luminous. My clothes hanging on
pegs, my white aprons and rubber boots, my
typewriter and tin box of biscuits, the big
sharp scissors on the table—all these familiar
things are touched with magic and make me
uneasy. Through the open door of the hut
comes the sweet sickish scent of new-mown
hay, mingling with the smell of disinfectants,
of Eau de Javel and iodoform, and wet mud
and blood. There is wet mud on my boots
and blood on my apron. I don't mind. It is
the scent of new-mown hay that makes me
uneasy. The little whimpering voice of a man
who is going to die in an hour or two comes
across the whispering grass from the hut next

51

door. That little sound I understand. It is like the mew of a wounded cat. Soon it will stop. It will stop soon after midnight. I know. I can tell. I go on duty at midnight, and he will die and go to Heaven soon after, lulled to sleep by the lullaby of the guns.

Far beyond him, out in the deep amorous night, I can hear the war going on. I hear the motor convoys rumbling down the road and the tramp of feet marching. I can tell the ambulances from the lorries and distinguish the wagons that carry provisions. Reinforcements are coming up along the road through the moonlit fields. The three-inch guns are pounding. All along the horizon they are pounding, pounding. But there will be no attack. The section is quiet. I know. I can tell. The cannonade is my lullaby. It soothes me. I am used to it. Every night it lulls me to sleep. If it stopped I could not sleep. I would wake with a start. The thin wooden walls of my cubicle tremble and the windows rattle a little. That, too, is natural. It is the whispering of the grass and the scent of new-mown hay that makes me nervous.

The war is the world, and this cardboard

house, eight by nine, behind the trenches, with a roof that leaks and windows that rattle, and an iron stove in the corner, is my home in it. I have lived here ever since I can remember. It had no beginning, it will have no end. War, the Alpha and the Omega, world without end—I don't mind it. I am used to it. I fit into it. It provides me with everything that I need, an occupation, a shelter, companions, a jug and a basin. When winter comes my stove is red hot, and I sit with my feet on it. When it rains I sleep under a mackintosh sheet with an umbrella over my pillow and a basin on my feet. Sometimes in a storm the roof blows off. Then I wait under the blankets for the old men to come and put it back again. Sometimes the Germans shell the cross roads beyond us or the town behind us, and the big shells pass over the hospital screaming. Then the surgeons in the operating hut turn up the collars of their white jackets, and we lift our shoulders round our ears. I don't mind—it is part of the routine. For companions there are, of course, the surgeons and the nurses and the old grizzled orderlies, but I have other companions more

53   C

intimate than these. Three in particular, a lascivious monster, a sick bad-tempered animal, and an angel ; Pain, Life and Death. The first two are quarrelsome. They fight over the wounded like dogs over a bone. They snarl and growl and worry the pieces of men that we have here; but Pain is the stronger. She is the greater. She is insatiable, greedy, vilely amorous, lustful, obscene—she lusts for the broken bodies we have here. Wherever I go I find her possessing the men in their beds, lying in bed with them; and Life, the sick animal, mews and whimpers, snarls and barks at her, till Death comes—the Angel, the peace-maker, the healer, whom we wait for, pray for—comes silently, drives Pain away, and horrid, snarling Life, and leaves the man in peace.

Lying in my bed, I listen to the great, familiar, muttering voice of the war and to the feeble, mewing, whimpering voice of Life, the sick bad-tempered animal, and to the loud triumphant guttural shouts of Pain plying her traffic in the hut next to me, where the broken bodies of men are laid out in rows with patches of moonlight on their coverlets. At midnight

I will get up and put on a clean apron and go across the grass to the sterilizing room and get a cup of cocoa. At midnight we always have cocoa in there next to the operating room, because there is a big table and boiling water. We push back the drums of clean dressings and the litter of soiled bandages, and drink our cocoa standing round the table. Sometimes there isn't much room. Sometimes legs and arms wrapped in cloths have to be pushed out of the way. We throw them on the floor—they belong to no one and are of no interest to anyone—and drink our cocoa. The cocoa tastes very good. It is part of the routine.

But the moonlight is like a pool of silver water on the floor, and the air is soft and the moon is floating, floating through the sky. In a dream I see her, in a crazy hurting dream. Lovely night, lovely lunatic moon, lovely scented love-sick earth—you are not true; you are not a part of the routine. You are a dream, an intolerable nightmare, and you recall a world that I once knew in a dream.

The mewing voice of the wounded cat dying in the shed next door to me is true.

He is my brother, that wounded cat. This also is true. His voice goes on and on. He tells the truth to me. He tells me what I know to be true. But soon—quite soon—I hope and think that his voice will stop. Now the monstrous mistress that he has taken to his bed has got him, but soon he will escape. He will go to sleep in her arms lulled by the lullaby of the pounding guns that he and I are used to, and then in his sleep the Angel will come and his soul will slip away. It will run lightly over the whispering grasses and murmuring trees. It will leap through the velvety dark that is tufted with the soft concussion of distant shells bursting from the mouths of cannon. It will fly up through the showery flares and shooting rockets past the moon into Heaven. I know this is true. I know it must be true.

How strange the moon is with its smooth cheeks. How I fear the whispering of the grasses and murmuring of the trees. What are they saying? I want to go to sleep to the old soothing lullaby of the cannon that rocks me—rocks me in my cradle—but they keep me awake with their awful whispering. I am

drowsy and drugged with heavy narcotics,
with ether and iodoform and other strong
odours. I could slee I could sleep with the
familiar damp smell of blood on my apron,
but the terrible scent of the new-mown hay
disturbs me. Crazy peasants came and cut it
while the battle was going on just beyond the
canal. Women and children came with pitchforks and tossed it in the sun. Now it lies
over the road in the moonlight, wafting its
distressing perfume into my window, bringing me waking dreams—unbearable, sickening, intolerable dreams—that interrupt the
routine.

Ah! The great gun down by the river is
roaring, is shouting. What a relief! That I
understand—that giant's voice. He is a friend
—another familiar, monstrous friend. I know
him. I listen every night for his roar. I long
to hear it. But it is dying away now. The
echo goes growling down the valley, and again
the trees and the grasses begin that murmuring and whispering. They are lying. It is a
lie that they are saying. There are no lovely
forgotten things. The other world was a
dream. Beyond the gauze curtains of the

tender night there is War, and nothing else but War. Hounds of war, growling, howling; bulls of war, bellowing, snorting; war eagles, shrieking and screaming; war fiends banging at the gates of Heaven, howling at the open gates of hell. There is War on the earth—nothing but War, War let loose in the world, War—nothing left in the whole world but War—War, world without end, amen.

I must change my apron now and go out into the moonlight. The sick man is still mewing. I must go to him. I am afraid to go to him. I cannot bear to go across the whispering grass and find him in the arms of his monstrous paramour. It is a night made for love, for love, for love. That is not true. That is a lie.

The peaked roofs of the huts stand out against the lovely sky. The moon is just above the abdominal ward. Next to it is the hut given up to gas gangrene, and next to that are the Heads. The Knees are on the other side, and the Elbows and the fractured Thighs. A nurse comes along carrying a lantern. Her white figure moves silently across the ground. Her lantern glows red in the moonlight. She goes into the gangrene hut that smells of swamp gas. She won't mind. She is used to it, just as I am. Pain is lying in there waiting for her. It is holding the damp greenish bodies of the gangrene cases in her arms. The nurse will try to get her out of those beds, but the loathesome creature will be too much for her. What can the nurse do against this she-devil, this Elemental, this Diva? She can straighten a pillow, pour drops out of a bottle, pierce a shrunken side with a needle. She can hold to lips a cup of cold water. Will that land her, too, in Heaven one day? I wonder; I doubt it. She is no longer a woman. She is dead already, just as I am—really dead, past resurrection. Her heart is dead. She killed it. She couldn't bear to feel it jumping in her side when Life, the sick animal, choked and rattled in her arms. Her ears are deaf; she deafened them. She could not bear to hear Life crying and mewing. She is blind so that she cannot see the torn parts of men she must handle. Blind, deaf, dead—she is strong, efficient, fit to consort with gods and demons—a machine in-

59

habited by the ghost of a woman—soulless, past redeeming, just as I am—just as I will be.

There are no men here, so why should I be a woman? There are heads and knees and mangled testicles. There are chests with holes as big as your fist, and pulpy thighs, shapeless; and stumps where legs once were fastened. There are eyes—eyes of sick dogs, sick cats, blind eyes, eyes of delirium; and mouths that cannot articulate; and parts of faces—the nose gone, or the jaw. There are these things, but no men; so how could I be a woman here and not die of it? Sometimes, suddenly, all in an instant, a man looks up at me from the shambles, a man's eyes signal or a voice calls "Sister! Sister!" Sometimes suddenly a smile flickers on a pillow, white, blinding, burning, and I die of it. I feel myself dying again. It is impossible to be a woman here. One must be dead.

Certainly they were men once. But now they are no longer men.

There has been a harvest. Crops of men were cut down in the fields of France where they were growing. They were mown down with a scythe, were gathered into bundles, tossed about with pitchforks, pitchforked into wagons and transported great distances and flung into ditches and scattered by storms and gathered up again and at last brought here— what was left of them.

Once they were real, splendid, ordinary, normal men. Now they mew like kittens. Once they were fathers and husbands and sons and the lovers of women. Now they scarcely remember. Sometimes they call to me "Sister, Sister!" in the faint voices of far-away men, but when I go near them and bend over them, I am a ghost woman leaning over a thing that is mewing; and it turns away its face and flings itself back into the arms of Pain, its monster bedfellow. Each one lies in the arms of this creature. Pain is the mistress of each one of them.

Not one can escape her. Neither the very old ones nor the young slender ones. Their weariness does not protect them, nor their loathing, nor their struggling, nor their cursing. Their hideous wounds are no protection, nor the blood that leaks from their wounds on to the bedclothes, nor the foul odour of their festering flesh. Pain is attracted by these things. She is a harlot in the pay of War, and she amuses herself with the wreckage of men. She consorts with decay, is addicted to blood, cohabits with mutilations, and her delight is the refuse of suffering bodies.

You can watch her plying her trade here any day. She is shameless. She lies in their beds all day. She lies with the Heads and the Knees and the festering Abdomens. She never leaves them. Even when she has exhausted them, even when at last worn out with her frenzy they drop into a doze, she lies beside them, to tease them with her excruciating caresses, her pinches and twinges that make them moan and twist in sleep. At any hour of the day or night you can watch her deadly amours, and watch her victims struggling. The wards are full of these writhings and tossings, they are agitated as if by a storm with her obscene antics. But if you come at midnight—if you come with me now—you will see the wounded, helpless, go fast asleep in her arms. You will see them abandon themselves to deep sleep with her beside them in their beds. They hope to escape her in sleep and find their way back to the fields where they were growing, strong lusty men, before they were cut down.

She lies there to spoil their dreams. When they dream of their women and little children, of their mothers and sweethearts; when they dream that they are again clean, normal, real men, filled with a tender and lovely love for women, then she wakes them. In the dark she wakes them and tightens her arms round their shrivelled bodies. She strangles their cries. She pours her poisoned breath into their panting mouths. She squeezes their throbbing hearts in their sides. In the dark, in the dark she takes them; she takes them to herself and keeps them until Death comes, the gentle angel. This is true. I know. I have seen.

Listen. Do you hear him? He is still mewing like a cat, but very faintly, and the trees are still murmuring and the grasses whispering. I hear the sound of many large creatures moving behind the hedge. They are panting and snorting. A procession of motor lorries and ambulances is going heavily down the road. They pass slowly, lumbering along with their heavy loads, and through the huge laborious sound of their grinding wheels threads the whirr of a swift touring car. You can hear it coming in the distance. It rushes nearer. It dashes past with a scratching shriek of its Klaxon. It plunges down the road and is gone. Some officer hurrying on some terrible business, some officer with gold leaves on his hat and a sword on his hip, in a limousine, leaning back on his cushions, calculating the number of men needed to repair yesterday's damage, and the number of sandbags required to repair their ditches. He does not see the lovely night and the lovely moon, and the unseemly love affair that is going on between the earth and the moon. He does not notice that he has passed the gate of a hospital, or know that behind the hedge men are lying in the dark with patches of blood and patches of moonlight on their coverlets. He is blind, deaf, dead, as I am—another machine just as I am.

It is twelve o'clock. The nurse has disappeared. She has left her lantern outside my door. There is no one to be seen. Nothing moves in the moonlight. But the earth is trembling, and the throbbing of the guns is the throbbing of the pulse of the War; world without end.

Listen! The whimpering mew of the wounded cat has stopped. There's not a sound except the whisper of the wind in the grass. Quick! Be quick! In a moment a man's spirit will escape, will be flying through the night past the pale, beautiful, sentimental face of the moon.

His name was tattooed on his arm, and the head of a woman life-size on his back. He himself might have been fashioned by Praxitiles, but some sailor in a North African port had dug needles of blue ink into the marble flesh of his arm, and written there the indelible words—Enfant de Malheur. He waved that slender member of his incredibly perfect Greek body in the nurse's face when she asked him his name, and said Voila ! with a biting sarcasm and a snarl of pointed white teeth. Then, glaring defiance, defying her to knife him in the back, he turned over and displayed his back to her. The face of a chocolate box beauty done in colours decorated its smooth surface. Her silly blue eyes stared up from between his fine flat shoulder blades and her full red lips smiled on his spinal cord. She was a trashy creature, a plump, coarse

66

morsel, no fit companion for this young prince
of darkness. He had race, distinction, an exquisite elegance, and, even in his battered
state, the savage grace of a panther. Not even
his wounds could disfigure him. The long
deep gash in his side made his smooth torso
seem the more incredibly fair and frail. The
loss of one leg rendered the other more exquisite with its round polished knee and slim
ankle.

He was one of a lot of some twenty Apaches
that had been brought in that morning. As
I remember them, they were all handsome
young men—these assassins, thieves, pimps
and traffickers in drugs—with sleek elastic
limbs, smooth polished skins and beautiful
bones. It was, if I remember rightly, only
about their heads that I noticed imperfection.
Their skulls were not quite right somehow,
nor the shape of their ears. Their foreheads
were low and receding, their jaws weak, and
their mouths betrayed depravity. Still they
were beautiful, beautiful as young leopards,
and they brought with them into the hospital
the strange morbid glamour of crime. But
the Enfant de Malheur was the most beautiful

of them all.　He had the face of an angel.

They were exiles, and they belonged to the Battalions D'Afrique that had been put into the line two days before on the eve of an attack.　Excellent troops of assault, these young Parisian criminals who had been sentenced to penal servitude for life and conscripted in the army of North Africa; but no good for holding the line or for anything else, so the General told me.　No stamina, no powers of endurance; but they were born killers and they went over the top when the signal was given like wolf-hounds suddenly unleashed.　Moreover, they knew that if they distinguished themselves in battle they would win back their freedom and become again at the end of the war, citizens of Paris.

Paris !　Montmartre !　The lighted cafés of the Place Blanche; the jingling, flashing, merry boulevards; these boys who lay like Greek gods in their beds recalled fantastically all the romantic tales that had ever been written by liars about the underworld of that most brilliant and seductive of capitals.　The cunning camouflage of their beauty made it all seem true.　The wild breath of false romance

swept down the huts over their beds. And
they lay in their beds, glaring, defiant, suspicious, expecting, so it seemed, to be attacked, assassinated or robbed in their beds
at any moment by any one of us.

Their arrival had created something of a
sensation in the hospital. The line had been
held for the last few weeks by regiments of
territorials, the "old ones," as we called them;
and we had received for many days nothing
but greybeards. Fathers and grandfathers.
"Vieux Pères," good troops they made for
holding the line in the wet winter weather.
They simply sat there doggedly in the cold,
the mud and the wet, enduring the war and
getting rheumatism in their old joints week
after week. So the arrival of this gang of
reckless, noisy, sardonic and suspicious cut-
throats was a pleasant diversion. But the
Medicin Chef wasn't pleased. He divided
them up carefully, put only two, or at the
most three, in each hut, and turned the
nurses out of the operating room, for when
these lovely beings were laid out in their
immaculate beauty on the operating table and
the ether mask was put over their proud

depraved, contemptuous faces, a stream of
language of such foulness spurted from their
chiselled lips that even the surgeons turned
sick.

Pim ignored this. Pim was in charge
of the Enfant de Malheur. She was the
daughter of an Archdeacon, and had been
brought up in a cathedral close in the North
of England, then had trained in Edinburgh.
She was an excellent nurse, very fastidious
about the care of the patients. Her blue uniform was always stiffly starched, her cap and
apron were immaculate; so was her smooth
severe Madonna face, with its childlike candid
eyes and thin quiet mouth. Pim didn't understand the word Apache. She didn't understand the Enfant de Malheur. She didn't, I
believe, notice that he was beautiful. She was
interested in his wounds and in saving his
life. She had come to the front to nurse the
French because she had been told that they
needed nurses more in the French army than
in England; but she was not interested in
Frenchmen, nor in any man. She knew no
men. She knew only her patients. And she
fought for their lives grimly, quietly, with her

thin gentle lips pressed tight together when
the crisis came. So she did not look at her
young Apache with curiosity, and she did not
know why he glared at her or why he gave a
start and leapt sideways in his bed when she
approached him. She made no attempt at
understanding his queer argot, and was unaware when he insulted her. She quite simply
continued to look after him with complete
serenity. She simply went on handling his
dangerous body with the perfectly assured
impersonal gentleness of an excellent surgical
nurse—washing him, dressing his wounds, giving him injections, enemas and bed pans, as if
she were at home in Edinburgh at work under
the eye of the most exacting of Scotch surgeons.

It was Guerin who understood that the
pain-racked body of the Enfant de Malheur
was as dangerous as an unexploded bomb.
Guerin was an orderly with the rank of corporal, and he shared with Pim the responsi-
bility of the ward. He was a priest, mobilized
for the war; but we forgot this the greater
part of the time, because he was so efficient
as a nurse and looked so little like a priest in
his neat blue corporal's uniform with his

bright alert eyes looking out through his pince nez. Indeed, it was only when one of Pim's patients died that we remembered that Guerin was a priest. Then Pim summoned him shyly and withdrew, leaving Guerin alone with the man who was dying.

Sometimes coming in I would find the little man kneeling by a bedside with a crucifix in his hands, and the sight of his neat compact figure and intent scholarly face would recall to me his other holy calling, and make me wonder. He was so unlike the big priest in the black cassock with the white head bandage, who strode through the hospital grounds swinging a walking stick, and who had won the Croix de Guerre with three palms for bravery in the field. Guerin had looked to me, when he first came to us, a bit of a prig. He had a slightly quizzical expression; his manner was dry and impersonal; but he was on duty at six in the morning, and although he was supposed to go off twelve hours later, he was usually there busy with Pim until late in the evening, swabbing tables, boiling up instruments, or writing letters to someone's dictation.

72

They were a very satisfactory couple.
They scarcely spoke to each other, but they
worked together as if they had been born
for this, and this alone—this silent, quick,
watchful, unceasing battle with death; this
struggle to save men's lives, by doing small
things accurately at the right moment—without fuss, without noise, without sign of
fatigue or hurry, or nervousness or despair.
Their hands, their feet, their eyes never
faltered and were never still. They made the
same calm, quick, exact movements, took no
unnecessary steps, left nothing undone. Yes,
a curiously harmonious pair, this tall English-
woman and small sturdy Frenchman. But
Guerin did more than Pim did, because he
understood more and had more to do. He
believed in the Holy Catholic Church and the
Remission of Sins and the Life Everlasting.
He had set himself a task that he never men-
tioned. These wounded were not only his
countrymen, they were his children, and he
considered himself responsible for their im-
mortal souls.

So he frowned and his small sharply-cut
features took on a look of added sharpness

and his keen eyes grew suddenly alert when the stretcher-bearers brought the Enfant de Malheur into the ward. He didn't interfere with Pim, but he watched. He didn't warn her or try to stop her, or keep her away from the lovely Greek god whom he knew to be one of the damned and a fiend out of hell; but when she leaned over the beautiful fierce chiselled face he was always on the watch. And so he saw what Pim, who didn't understand, couldn't see. He saw that this damné, this vile savage rat from the sewers of Paris, was puzzled, bewildered, intimidated by Pim's stolid impersonal gentleness. He saw him gradually stop jumping to one side of the bed and take to wriggling and squirming with acute discomfort under her candid gaze, and he heard him muttering and snarling under his breath with exasperation at the insufferable presence of this Madonna-like woman with the cold, white, calm face. Guerin understood how uncomfortable the Enfant de Malheur would be in the presence of the beautiful Mother of God, and he watched him wriggle to avoid Pim's cool maiden eyes. And so on the third day, when the Apache

beckoned Pim to come to him, Guerin was
even more surprised than Pim was, because he
knew that the wicked brute in the boy had
been tamed by the power of Pim's unconscious serenity. Pim approached calmly. She
was rather a stupid woman in some ways.
"What is it?" she asked in her virginal
English voice. "Que voulez-vous?" And
Guerin, listening, watchful still, but with his
tense face relaxed a little, heard the Apache
whisper as he pulled Pim down: "Come
close. I want to tell you something. I want
to tell you," said the child of misfortune into
Pim's clean white ear, "that I have never
deliberately killed a woman in my life."

And then Guerin heard Pim murmur
quietly in her stiff polite way, as if she were
interviewing some well-meaning but unfortu-
nate backsliding parishioner in the Deanery:
"I'm so glad to hear it." And then the fiend
out of hell, incarnate in the sewer rat with the
angel face, fell back on his pillows with a
sudden look of sharp self-disgust, and Pim
moved off down the ward about her business.

I don't think it occurred to her to wonder
what his phrase implied, or how many women

he had killed, as he would have called it, by accident, or how many men with intent. I don't believe she was aware of the immense compliment he had paid her, or of having gained any victory over him. She had no knowledge of vice or evil. She did not know that he was truly one of the damned, and that his heart was black and heavy with a sick black weight of fear that came sweeping over him in his new weakness, and so next day, when he began to be frightened, she was surprised by the wild gleams of fear that came and went in his eyes.

But Guerin knew. He was a student of men, and he knew that the Enfant de Malheur was his brother, and believed in what he himself believed, namely, in the Holy Catholic Church and the Life Everlasting, in God, and the Mother of God, and the Holy Son of God, against whom he had fought and blasphemed since the day he was born.

His condition, both physical and moral, grew rapidly worse after this. Symptoms of gangrene set in. A second amputation was necessary, high up the thigh, almost at the hip, and again Pim, who had followed her patient to the operating room, was told to go away. She refused. She stood there obstinately while streams of filth and obscenity spurted from his beautiful pale mouth— putrid psychic sewage of the underworld spouting from him like a fountain; but to the surgeon's embarrassed, irritated excuses she answered: "I don't understand his language, so what difference does it make?" and she took him back and put him gently to bed.

But when he came to after the operation, there was a new look in his eyes. Pim went white at the sight of it, and her hand, as she put the long saline needle into his side, trembled, and she went in search of Guerin.

"He is so frightened," she said, "he is so afraid to die. I can't bear it. We must save him, Guerin."

So they conspired to save him. There were forty beds in the hut, and they were all full; but those two—Pim and Guerin—without fuss multiplied themselves. No royal patient was ever nursed with greater care than our Enfant de Malheur, but he grew worse, and his fear grew worse. His fear increased until its presence filled the ward, and the old grey-

beards in their beds turned away their faces
and stopped their ears to hide from it.

He began to sweat terribly. He began to
toss and writhe. He began to smell bad.
Moods of blasphemous bravado alternated
with fits of uncontrollable panic. In the
middle of a curse his teeth would begin to
chatter. Then suddenly his eyes would start
from his head in terror, and he would shriek
for help and thrash out wildly till Pim came
to him or Guerin. Sometimes he sobbed like
a child in Pim's arms. More often he raged at
her, cursed her and Guerin and God. His bed
became a centre of obscenity. Foul odours,
foul words, foul matter swirled round him,
and always there was that terror in his eyes,
and the sweat pouring down his body that
was greenish now as if covered with slime.
The tattooed lady smiled through the slime
on his back, and he would wave his wasted
arm and hit out with it, and the big letters
seemed to shout to Pim down the ward : Enfant de Malheur !

Finally he could not bear her near him,
could not bear the sight of her near his bed or
the touch of her hands. One afternoon he

yelled at her to go away, leave him alone. She had maintained so far her stolid serenity, but at that she broke down. I found her behind her screen at the end of the ward with her shoulders shaking, her face twisting. It was nine o'clock in the evening. I told her to go off duty at once.

"But he is going to die in the night," she whispered.

"I know."

"And he is terribly frightened."

"I know."

"His fear is so ugly. It frightens me and the others, all the old men. We must do something. Can't we do something?"

"Perhaps Guerin can do something. You and I, what can we do?"

"If only he weren't so sane. If only he didn't realise. But his fever seems to have sharpened his wits. He knows he is going to die. He never forgets for a second. He hasn't had a wink of sleep. Dying usually slows down, blurs everything, brings a merciful dullness; but for him there is no such mercy. His nerves are live wires. Morphine has no effect. I've given him extra doses. No good,

79

not a bit of good. But he must have relief, I tell you. This is impossible." Her face had a slightly crazed look. "I tell you I am ready to give him any amount of stuff. I'll do anything to put an end to it."

I said, "Come along, Pim. You can't kill your patient. Come now at once. You're doing no good here." What he wants, I said to myself, is to be convinced that he has nothing to be afraid of. But suppose I tried to convince him that there was nothing to fear, no God, no crucified Christ waiting, no everlasting life stretching ahead of him, nothing but nothingness, I could never convince him—never. I had no power over his fear.

Guerin met me at the door of the hut as I was going out with Pim. He was polishing his eyeglasses.

"I would like permission to spend the night in the ward," he said in his quick way, adjusting his pince nez on his pointed nose.

"Very well, Guerin. You've been on duty all day, and you'll be on all day to-morrow, remember."

"Don't worry about that," he said briefly, dismissing us both with a wave of his hand.

"Can I do nothing, Guerin?" Pim asked meekly.

"Nothing, Mademoiselle."

They looked at each other. Then she looked down the ward to where the boy was lying and her mouth contracted. We could distinguish from our distance the terrified eyes.

"What is he afraid of?" she asked, shuddering.

"Of hell, Mademoiselle," said Guerin. And suddenly, as if he had heard us, some power jerked the boy off his pillow, and his arms shot out in front of him. "Je ne meurs pas," he cried; "Je ne meurs pas. Je ne voudrais pas mourir." I hurried Pim away.

When I went back, Guerin was on his knees by the boy's bed reading in low rapid tones from a little book. The Enfant de Malheur was not listening. He was quite unaware of him. He was entirely and horribly absorbed by another presence that seemed to be attacking him as an octopus attacks with a dozen arms. He was writhing in the unseen clutches. He was dodging and twisting and hissing at the thing through clenched teeth, and his eyes darted this way and that like beings separate from himself, possessed by a panic of their own.

I went from bed to bed attending to the old grumbling ones and trying not to look, but I could hear his fear increasing. Its tempo grew audibly more rapid, more frantic. His invisible enemy seemed to be going for him now in rushes and leaps of increasing fury. I hurried through my work, scolding in whispers the old men who were annoyed by his noise and troubled by his fear. I rattled my basins and kettles, making a noise of my own to distract them. But I could hear the boy's sobbing breath, hear him choking and shuddering, and every few seconds his voice would burst from his suffocating chest in a wail of defiant terror, and once he went off into a peal of hysterical laughter.

Guerin's low voice went on through it all. His words followed each other rapidly, in a monotone, in a level directed chant. He was aiming them straight at the head of the sweating terror-struck creature beside him. He paid no attention to me. Neither of them was aware of me. I hurried past them and went out.

I had a great deal to do. I went from hut to hut. I gave piqures and medicines and drinks, adjusted bandages and pillows, filled hot water bottles. I busied myself busily, making an unnecessary fuss over my duties, and tried to absorb myself in relieving the shadowy suffering forms that lay so patiently, murmuring their gratitude. I was greedy for their gratitude. I wanted badly to be comforted. But I had a feeling of sickening suspense and miserable futility. I could not forget those two. But I thought of them as three. I caught myself saying to myself : "There is Guerin and the Enfant de Malheur and another. It isn't just a case of one man fighting the panic of another. That's what you call it. That's what you want to believe it is. But there is something there that inspires the panic. Something else, something immense. The boy is a worm; the priest is an insignificant little man. But there are huge invisible things assaulting that noisome bed. What? The powers of darkness?"

"Nonsense," I said to myself. I was adjusting the pulleys of a fracture case. "There are no dark powers abroad in the world. There is

only death and pain and human evil and puny
human remorse. The boy is a murderer, a
thief, a vile rat, and he knows it; that's all,
but soon it will all be over. Soon he'll be
nothing, nothing. You know all the rest is
silly superstition. If Guerin didn't happen to
be a Catholic priest he wouldn't take it so
hard."

But even the quiet huts full of sleeping
men seemed to be filled with mystery, and I
hurried to get back to that other one across
the way, where I knew an immense struggle
was going on. I couldn't bear not to see what
was happening. I was afraid to go back, but
fascinated, haunted, allured. "If Guerin didn't
happen to be a priest he would be as useless
as you are in the face of this," I said to myself.
But could even Guerin do anything? Who
was Guerin? A good orderly, a conscientious
little man who believed in old legends. Very
well, very well. Put it that the power of an
aged belief was being put to the test in that
ugly hut. I must see; I must know. I was
devoured with curiosity.

My round took me two hours. It was midnight when I got back to them. Guerin was

in the same position, on his knees, but he was praying now with a crucifix in his lifted hands and his eyes were closed. His face showed signs of great fatigue; it was tight and strained, but it wore a curious expression. And this expression was so concentrated that it seemed to come from his face and shoot upward like a shaft of dark light. I cannot describe it otherwise. His voice, too, had gained in power; it was low, level, and penetrating, but there were undertones in it that made one's nerves tingle. "Dieu qui nous regarde, ayez pitié. Dieu le Saveur, je vous supplie—"

The Enfant de Malheur, I saw with a sickening catch in my side, had changed too, and the change was dreadful. I had hoped. What had I hoped? In his growing exhaustion and terror he had a look of madness. He was almost unrecognisable. There was a devilish hatred on his clammy face, a vile frantic fury, as well as an agony of terror. His fury seemed directed toward Guerin and the crucifix, while his terror was concentrated on something straight in front of him. His lips were twisted into a malevolent and hideous snarl ; his eyes were the eyes of a suffering lunatic; they shot sullen sidelong looks of wild vindictiveness at the crucifix. As I passed he gave a vicious leap toward the foot of the bed, flung his tortured body past the priest's head, hit out at the Christ with his fist, and, grinding his teeth, yelled out a hideous curse into the shadows. Guerin's voice became audible again an instant later : "Dieu, notre seul espoir—Dieu, notre Sauveur." The old men groaned and muttered, half waking.

At two o'clock the struggle was still going on and the situation seemed to me at first unchanged except that the apache and the priest were both fainting with exhaustion; but I noticed presently that they had come to closer grips with each other. Guerin, still on his knees, was talking now with his mouth close to the boy's head, talking with a breathless intensity, saying apparently the same thing over and over, as if he were trying to drive home into that maddened brain a single important fact, and it seemed to me that through his terror the dying boy was listening in spite of himself. His attention was now very evidently divided between the death that menaced him at the foot of his bed and the

voice that spoke in his ear. He was still
fighting, but while he fought he listened
reluctantly, fearful of allowing his attention to
be distracted from his awful antagonist for a
second, but nevertheless compelled to pay
attention. And his antagonist seemed to have
withdrawn a little. The beast was crouching,
was cowering now, so it seemed to me. I
stood at a distance under the lamp that hung
from the peaked roof and watched. Guerin
was panting for breath as if he had been running in a long race. But he seemed to be win-
ning: he seemed to have pushed back a little
that dark power. The boy was undoubtedly
listening to his rapid, determined, insistent
voice. The power in it was reaching him.
What power? Guerin's, you fool, I said to myself, but what powers did Guerin have to
draw on. He had been at it now for four
hours. Could he last out, keep it up? Keep
up what? What, after all, was he doing? Was
he telling the sewer rat lies to get him quiet?
But how could he go on lying and lying?
What power lay in tricks and falsehood to
rout that awful terror? If Guerin failed he
would, I caught myself thinking, be proved a

liar; but if he won, what then? And just at
that moment I saw the boy break away from
Guerin's voice and plunge with a shriek back
into his agony and begin to writhe again as
if grappling with a monster; and I almost ran
to the door, sick with horror and disappoint-
ment.

"He has failed," I said to myself. "Guerin
has failed." And I hurried away with my
lantern through the bitter air, making excuses
for him. "It's too long, it's too much. He's
been at it all night. No man on earth could
keep it up at that pitch of intensity." I
stopped, stood staring down at my lantern.
"But he'd almost got him," I whispered, "and
now he's lost him again." But had he? I
turned round. Suppose Guerin had given
up? I went running back. "I couldn't bear
that, Guerin," I whispered. "I couldn't bear
to see you beaten;" I felt half suffocated as I
crept to the door and looked in again.

Guerin had not relaxed or changed his
position; he was still praying, praying. His
words came to my ears like the soft raps of a
small muffled hammer, hammering away,
hammering and hammering.

And as I went on my rounds again, from hut to hut and bed to bed, I kept hearing Guerin's voice, hammering away, hammering away at the gates of Heaven for the sake of the poor Enfant de Malheur. I knew now that nothing could stop him, that he would never give in, but I knew, too, that his time was getting short. The boy couldn't last much longer. Soon he would die. Would he die in terror, aware of his unutterable vileness? Would Guerin be forced to see that happen? Would he be proved to himself to be a liar?

I felt cold and very tired. The sky was beginning to pale. It was four o'clock, the hour when life beats most feebly in the bodies of men. I went from hut to hut again, listening for the little sounds of uncertain fluttering life. Was this one slipping away or that one? " No one, no one else must die to-night," I kept saying to myself. " There is only one death here to-night." Then I turned towards Guerin's hut. It stood ungainly and ugly in the half light, a wooden shelter through which many men had passed, some to go home, some to be buried in our cemetery where the wooden crosses stood so modestly above the ground. None of them stayed with us. All were lost to us. They passed like shadows. I could not remember them. They had no names, no faces in my memory. Who were they? What were they? What had become of them? I did not know. I knew nothing about them; I knew nothing of the dead or the living. I felt cold. I felt dreadfully cold as I approached the door, but as I entered I was aware that a strange hush had come into the ward, and through it I heard the old men breathing, and a young voice talking. It was the Enfant de Malheur who was speaking. He was talking to Guerin in a small weak child's voice, and Guerin was kneeling beside him with the sweat pouring down his face. I saw Guerin take his handkerchief from his pocket and wipe his forehead, but he did not take his eyes from the boy's eyes while he did this. They were both quiet; Guerin was very, very quiet, but the boy was sobbing a little, He was confessing his sins. He was pouring out all his dark, secret, haunting memories into Guerin's ears and sobbing with relief. I turned and tip-toed out again, and stood for awhile against the wall of the hut, trembling.

I went back at five. I could not keep away. I went back half through my round. I knew that I must not miss the last act of the drama that was playing itself out so quietly on that ugly narrow bed. I knew that I would never again in this world see anything so mysterious·

The dawn was filtering into the long wooden hut, filling it with the twilight of morning. The old men in their beds lay asleep. I looked down the long row apprehensively with a last catch at the heart. Was it over? Had Guerin really won ? No, it was not over yet. Yes, yes, he had won. There they were, the two of them, and the boy's white face was smiling above smoothed sheets. His eyes were closed. He lay relaxed, at peace, happy, and a small crumpled figure was still kneeling beside his bed and a low voice was praying again: "Jesu —Dieu—Sauveur qui nous regard." And I knew that the Enfant de Malheur was listening. I knew that he could hear, because he moved a little, and touched the priest's arm, half opened his eyes, and smiled as I watched him.

He died at six o'clock, holding Guerin by the hand. Then Guerin loosed his hand, and crossed the boy's two hands on his wasted chest over the small crucifix, and rose from his knees and walked stiffly to the door.

The sun was rising. He staggered a little as he came out into the fresh morning air. I stood beside him. He began polishing his pince-nez. The sky was crimson behind the wooden sheds. Suddenly, softly, it filled with golden light. Great luminous bands spread up and out like a fan from the horizon. I looked at Guerin, so small, so crumpled, so exhausted. He did not look at all like a man of God. He looked like a book-worm, a bit of a prig, an insignificant little man.

"What does it mean, Guerin?" I asked. "It was like a miracle; but what does it mean?"

"He is safe." Guerin said briefly. Then he adjusted his pince-nez, gave me a quick sharp look, and turned away to his own quarters.

THE stretcher bearers staggered under his weight when they brought him along through the sunlight to the operating room. They put him down for a moment on the ground outside the operating hut and wiped the sweat off their old foreheads. It was a hot summer's day. The sector was quiet. The attack that had filled the hospital two days before had fizzled out. Now only occasional ambulances lurched in at the gate, bringing men who had been missed by the stretcher bearers, left out for a couple of nights on No Man's Land, or been wounded unnecessarily by stray bullets after the big push was over. This man had come up over the horizon alone, a red giant, brought unconscious through the summer afternoon in a battered Ford, and deposited like a log on our doorstep, solitary character of some obscure incident in the aftermath of battle. He lay on the ground like a felled ox, a bull mortally wounded, breathing noisily.

His head was bound with a soiled bandage; his eyes were closed; his bruised mouth was open. Thick tufts of red hair pushed through the head bandage. There was dried blood round his immense rough lips. His huge red face was dark and blurred. He was covered with dust. He looked as if he had been rolling in a dirty field like some farm animal. He was a man of the soil, of the dark earth, with the heavy power of the earth in him. The bright sun shining on his massive unconscious bulk made the darkness of his lost consciousness visible. He seemed to lie deep, distant, withdrawn in a shadowy abyss. His spirit—brother spirit of ox and bullock and all beasts of the field—was deep asleep, in that sleep which is the No Man's Land of the soul, and from which men seldom come back. But his immense body continued, in spite of his absence to hum and drum like a dynamo, like a machine whose tremendous power takes time to run down, and his breath came whistling and spurting through his rough bruised lips like escaping steam.

94

The old stretcher-bearers lifted him again grunting, and brought him in to us and hoisted him with difficulty on to the narrow white table, in the white room full of glistening bottles and shining basins and silvered instruments, among the white-coated surgeons and nurses. His head hung over one end of the table, and his feet over the other, and his great freckled arms hung helpless and heavy down at either side. Thick curling bunches of red hair, wiry and vigorous, grew out of his enormous chest. We stripped his body. It lay inert, a mountainous mass, with the rough-hewn brick-red face tipped back. His sightless face reminded one of the face of a rock in a sandstone quarry, chiselled with a pick-axe, deeply gashed. His closed eyes were caves under bushy cliffs, his battered mouth a dark shaft leading down into a cavern where a hammer was beating.

Because he was so big, his helplessness was the more helpless. But one could feel life pounding powerfully in his body—senseless life, pounding on, pumping air into his lungs, keeping his heart going. Yes, he would be hard to kill, I thought. Even a bullet in the head hadn't killed him.

95

I counted his pulse. It was strong and steady.

"Shot through the mouth. Revolver bullet lodged in the brain." Monsieur X was reading the ticket that had been pinned to the man's blanket in the dressing station behind the front line.

But how? I wondered. How queer, I thought. Shot in the mouth—through the roof of the mouth. He must have been asleep in the trench with his mouth open. And I imagined him there, sprawling in the muddy ditch, an exhausted animal with his great stupid mouth open; and I saw a figure crawl in beside him and put the barrel of a revolver between his big yellow teeth. Fool, I thought. You fool—you big hulking brute beast—going to sleep like that in utter careless weariness.

But no, it was impossible. In this war such things didn't happen. Men were killed haphazard—maimed, torn to pieces, scattered by shell fire, plugged full of shrapnel, hit square sometimes by rifle bullets, but not shot neatly through the roof of the mouth with a revolver.

They were whispering as they bent over

him. Monsieur X frowned, pinched his lips together, looked down at the great, gentle unconscious carcase sideways.

" But how?" I asked. "Who?"

"Himself. He shot himself through the mouth. It's a suicide."

"Suicide !" I echoed the word vaguely, as if it contained a mystery. There was something queer, out of the ordinary, about it, shocking to the surgeons and orderlies. They were ashamed, worried, rather flustered. "But why suicide?" I asked, suddenly aware of the extraordinary fact that a personal tragedy had lifted its head above the dead level of mass destruction. It was this that shocked them.

He's not young, I thought, cutting the bandage round the rough unconscious head with its shock of matted red hair. A peasant, probably—very stupid—an ox of a man.

"Why suicide?" I asked aloud.

"Panic," answered Monsieur briefly. "Fear —he tried to kill himself from fear of being killed. They do sometimes."

"This one didn't."

"No, he didn't succeed, this big one. He

ought to be dead. The bullet is here just under the skull. It's gone clean through his brain. Any other man would be dead. He's strong, this big one.

"You'll extract it?"

"But certainly."

"And he will live?"

"Perhaps."

"And what then?"

"He'll be court-martialed and shot, Madame, for attempted suicide."

They were strapping his iron arms and legs to the narrow table. Someone lifted his heavy head. Someone pulled his great bulk into position and bound him to the table with strong leather bands.

"Don't do it!" I shouted suddenly. "Leave him alone." I was appalled by his immense helplessness.

They went on with their business of getting him ready. They didn't hear me. Perhaps I had not shouted aloud.

"You don't understand," I cried. "You've made a mistake. It wasn't fear. It was something else. He had a reason, a secret. It's locked there in his chest. Leave him alone with it. You can't bring him back now to be shot again."

But they clapped the ether mask over his face, stifling his enormous stentorious breathing, and with that he began to struggle—the dying ox. Life, roused by the menace of the suffocating gas, sprang up in him again— gigantic, furious, suffering, a baited bull. It began plunging in him, straining, leaping to get out of his carcase and attack its enemies. A leather thong snapped, a fist shot out, knocking over bottles and basins. There was a crash, a tinkle of broken glass, a scramble of feet, and suddenly through the confusion I heard a thin soft anguished voice cry as if from a great distance, "Rosa, Rosa!" It came from his chest; it sounded like the voice of a man lost in a cave. It came from under his heaving side where the bushy hair grew thick and strong—a hollow heartbroken voice, issuing from his blind unconscious mouth, in a long cry—"Rosa, Rosa!"

Twice again he called Rosa before they could clap the ether mask down again on his face.

It was a neat operation and entirely suc-

cessful. They took the bullet out of the top
of his head, bandaged his head up again, and
carried him away through the sunny afternoon
to be put to bed.

"He will surely die in the night," I said to
myself, and I went again and again in the
night to see if, happily, he were dead; but always, standing beside the shadow of his great
bulk, I could hear him breathing, and once I
thought I heard sighing on his shrouded lips
the name of the woman—Rosa.

"He can't live," the night nurse said.

"He can't die," I whispered to myself.
" Life is too strong in him, too hard to kill."

He was much better next day. I found him
sitting up in bed in a clean pink flannel night
shirt, staring in front of him. He didn't answer when I said "Good morning," or take
any notice of me. He hadn't spoken to any one
during the day, the nurse told me, but he was
very obedient and ate his soup quietly, "as
good as gold," she said he was. "A remark-
able case," Monsieur X said. "He ought to be
dead." But there he was sitting up eating
his meals with an excellent appetite.

"So he knows what will happen?" I asked,

following the surgeon to the door.

"But certainly. They all know. Everyone in the army knows the penalty."

The suicide did not turn his head or look in my direction. He was still staring straight ahead of him when I came back and stood at the foot of his bed.

Who are you? I wondered, and who is Rosa? And what can I do? How can I help you? And I stood there waiting, miserably spellbound by the patient brute who at last turned on me from his cavernous eyes a look of complete understanding, and then looked heavily away again.

That night when the orderly was dozing and the night nurse was going on her round from hut to hut, he tore the bandage from his head. She found him with his head oozing on the pillow, and scolded him roundly. He didn't answer. He said nothing. He seemed not to notice. Meekly, docile as a friendly trusting dog, he let her bandage him up again, and the next morning I found him again sitting up in his bed in his clean head bandage staring in front of him with that dark look of dumb subhuman suffering. And the next night the same thing happened, and the next, and the next. Every night he tore off his bandage, and then let himself be tied up again.

"If his wound becomes infected he'll die," said Monsieur X, angrily.

"That's what he's trying to do," I answered. "Kill himself again before they can shoot him," I added, "to save them the trouble."

I dared not speak to the man whom I thought of day and night as Rosa, having never learned his name, and he never spoke to me or any one. His eyes, which he now always turned on me when I came in, forbade me to speak to him. They stared into mine with the understanding of a brute mortally wounded, who is not allowed to die, so I went to the General, and, actuated by some hysterical impulse, pleaded for the man's life.

"But, Madame, we have epidemics of suicide in the trenches. Panic seizes the men. They blow their brains out in a panic. Unless the penalty is what it is—to be court-martialed and shot—the thing would spread. We'd find ourselves going over the top with battalions of dead men. The same penalty applies to men who wound themselves. That's the favourite device of a coward. He puts the muzzle of his rifle on his foot and fires."

I argued. I explained that this man was not afraid of being killed, but of not being killed, that his luck was out when the enemy missed him; that he had been kept waiting too long, had shot himself in despair because the Germans wouldn't shoot him; and a woman called Rosa let him down, or perhaps she died. Perhaps he simply wanted to go to her.

"He must have had a letter in the trenches —a letter from Rosa or about her. He's not a young man. He is forty or more—an enormous brute with red hair and hands like hams. A farmer probably. One of those slow plodding gentle brute men, faithful as dogs. His voice was broken-hearted, high and hollow like a child's voice, when he called to her. Like a child that is lost. 'Rosa! Rosa!' If you'd heard him.

"And here you are with your military regulations asking me to save him for you so that you can shoot him. You expect us to tie up

his head every night and prevent his dying so
that you can march him off to trial and stand
him up against a wall."

But what was the good of arguing against
army regulations? We were at war. The
General could do nothing. The man must be
made an example, so that these epidemics of
suicide could be kept in check.

I didn't dare go back to Rosa. I went to the
door of the hut and called the nurse. Down
in the centre of the long row of beds I could
see his great shoulders and his huge bandaged
head. He looked like a monstrous baby in his
white bonnet and pink flannel shirt. But I
knew that his big haggard eyes were staring,
and I remembered that his face had been a
little paler each day, that it was not brick
colour any more, but the colour of wax, that
his cheek bones stood out like shelves.

He's killing himself in spite of us all, I
thought. He's succeeding. It's hard work,
it takes patience, but he's doing it. Given a
chance, he'll pull it off. Well, he'll have his
chance. I almost laughed. I had been a fool
to go to the General and plead for his life.
That was the last thing he wanted me to do

for him. That was just the wrong thing.

I spoke to the nurse who was going on duty for the night.

"When Rosa pulls off his bandage to-night, leave it off," I said abruptly.

She looked at me a minute hesitating. She was highly trained. Her traditions, her professional conscience, the honour of her calling loomed for a moment before her, then her eyes lighted. "All right," she said.

I thought when I stood at the foot of Rosa's bed next morning and found him staring at me that I detected a look of recognition in his eyes, perhaps even a faint look of gratitude, but I could not be sure. His gaze was so sombre, so deep, that I could not read it, but I could see that he was weaker. Perhaps it was his increased pallor that made his eyes so enormously dark and mysterious. Towards evening he grew delirious, but he tore off his bandage all the same, in the middle of the night. He managed to do that. It was his last effort, his last fumbling desperate and determined act. His fixed idea prevailed through his delirium, his will triumphed. It was enough. He was unconscious next morning and he died two days later, calling in his weary abysmal heart for Rosa, though we could not hear him.

PART TWO

THE SOMME

THE CITY IN THE DESERT

WHAT is this city that sprawls in the shallow
valley between the chalk hills ? Why are its
buildings all alike, gaunt wooden sheds with
iron roofs? Why are there no trees, no gardens, no pleasant places? The sheds are
placed on top of the muddy ground like
boxes, row after row of them, with iron rails
down the centre where the main street of the
town should be. But there are no streets.
There are only tracks in the mud and wooden
walks laid across the mud from one shed to
the other, and a railway line.

I see no children playing anywhere. The
wind brings no sound of laughter from the
place, or splendid shouting, no sound of any
kind. Silent men in couples are carrying
heavy bundles between them from one shed
to the other, heads down to the wind. The
small white figure of a solitary woman is

crossing a wide open space. She is slipping in the mud. Her white dress is fluttering. The place is immense and empty, new and still and desolate. But the naked wet hills are throbbing. There's a noise of distant booming as if the sea were breaking against their sides.

You tell me there is no sea over there. But the roar? Surely there are waves breaking, and this desert is wet as if a great wave had just receded, leaving the muddy bottom of the earth uncovered. A bare sea bottom, strewn with bits of iron, coils of wire, stones. No sign of life, no fish fossils, or rotting sea-weed, no plant of any kind, not a blade of green; a dead sea must have lain here.

Whoever built this city on this slippery waste, built it quick, at ebb tide, between tides, to serve some queer purpose between low and high tide. They put up these sheds in a hurry, covered them with sheets of corrugated iron, pinned them to the mud somehow, anyhow, knowing that a roaring surge would rise again, come rolling back over the hills to carry them away again. Then all these new buildings, all this timber and these sheets of iron will be broken up, and will rush down in a torrent.

Down where ? How do I know. I'm lost.
I've lost my way. The road was slippery.
There were no landmarks. The village I used
to know at the cross-roads was gone. Everything was sliding in the mud and all the villages that I knew here once on a time had
slipped clean out of sight, and now all the men
and horses in the world with wagons and
motor lorries seem to be pouring after them
into a gulf. The earth is a greased slide, tilted
up and shaking. And the men who built this
place knew evidently that there was danger of
the face of the earth itself slipping —for look
over there on that hill-side and that one—
they've tied the earth down with wire. You
see those intersecting bands of wire, looking
like a field of tangled iron weeds and iron
thistles? That is evidently to keep the mud
from slipping away.

Queer, isn't it? This new city where there
once was a snug town huddled round a
church with cafés, little tables under the
trees, schoolboys in black pinafores playing on
the church steps. The inn, I remember, was
famous for its cuisine. What has become of
the fat landlord who watched the plump suc-

culent fowls turning on a spit and dripping? Now, there's this place that looks like a mining town or a lumber camp, only it can't be. There's not a tree to be seen, north, south, east, or west, nothing but mud glistening. It's very queer, I say. That flimsy gate there with a banner across it as if for a celebration, with H.O.E. 32 on it in big black letters, and a flag flying, and those red crosses painted on the iron roofs of the buildings. H.O.E. 32 must be the name of the place; but why such a name? What does it mean?

Perhaps there has been a new flood, since Noah, and you and I slept through it. Perhaps a new race of men has been hatched out of the mud, hatched like newts, slugs, larvæ of water beetles. But slugs who know horribly, acutely, that they have only a moment to live in between flood tides and so built this place quickly, a silly shelter against the wrath of God, and gave it a magic hieroglyphic name, and put the name on a banner and hoisted a flag, and then put those red crosses up there, tipped skywards. Everything showy in the place points skywards, is designed to catch an eye in the sky, a great angry eye.

Otherwise it seems a secret place, vast, spread out, bare but secret; and some strange industry, some dreadful trade is evidently being carried on here in the wet desert, where a flood has passed and another flood will come.

The workers have a curious apprehensive look with their big secretive bundles. They may be smugglers. Certainly some shameful merchandise is being smuggled in here from the shore that you say is not the shore of the sea. If the booming noise beyond the hills were the roar of waves breaking, one would say that these old men were gangs of beach-combers, bringing up bundles of wreckage; that they go out across the mud under cover of the night to hunt in the backwash. You can see from the way they move that the stuff is valuable and breakable. They come out of the sheds cautiously and go carefully along the narrow board walks, two by two, with the heavy brown bundles swinging between them. They are as careful as they can be. They seem to be old men. They stagger under the weight that swings from their arms and their old shoulders cower as if under the lash of an invisible whip ; but they go up and down the long rows of sheds, patiently, carefully, gently, taking small careful steps.

You say that these bundles are the citizens of the town? What do you mean? Those heavy brown packages that are carried back and forth, up and down, from shed to shed, those inert lumps cannot be men. They are delivered to this place in closed vans and are unloaded like sacks and are laid out in rows on the ground and are sorted out by the labels pinned to their covers. They lie perfectly still while they are carried back and forth, up and down, shoved into sheds and pulled out again. What do you mean by telling me that they are men?

Why, if they are men, don't they walk? Why don't they talk? Why don't they protest? They lie perfectly still. They make no sound, They are covered up. You do not expect me to believe that inside that roll there is a man, and in that one, and in that one?

Ah, dear God, it's true! Look! Look through the window. The old men are undoing the bundles inside this shed. Look, there's a face and there's an arm hanging down crooked, and there I see a pair of boots sticking out at one end of a bundle.

But how queer they are! How strangely they lie there. They are not the usual shape. They only remind one of men. Some, to be sure, are wearing coats, and some have on iron hats, but all of them seem to be broken and tied together with white rags. And how dirty they are! The mud is crusted on them. Their boots are lumps of mud. Their faces are grey and wet as if modelled of pale mud. But what are those red, rusty stains on their dirty white rags? They have gone rusty lying out there in the mud, in the backwash. Ah, what a pity. Here is one without an arm, and another and another, and there, dear God, is one without a face! Oh! Oh! What are the old men doing to them? They are pulling off their clothes, uncovering the dreadful holes in their sides. Come away, come away from the window. I know now. There is no need to sneak up and stare at them.

They are lost men, wrecked men, survivors from that other world that was here before the flood passed this way, washed up against the shore of this world again by the great backwash. They thought that they had done with it, thought it was over and done with, thought they had left it for ever. But they've been brought here, brought back again to this city of refuge called H.O.E. 32, that sprawls under the angry Eye of God. Bundled into vans they were, all mangled and broken, carried back over the sliding mud through that flimsy gate where the flag is flapping, to be saved. To be hauled about and man-handled, to have their broken, bleeding nakedness uncovered, to have their bodies cut again with knives and their deep wounds probed with pincers, and to have the breath choked back in their sobbing lungs again, so that they may be saved for this world.

How strange it must look to them when they open their eyes! There are no trees anywhere. There is no shelter, except under the iron roofs. The place is new and still and desolate. But the wind is howling over the wet desert, and the old men who go carefully up and down with their heavy oblong bundles, stop and listen to the booming sound beyond the hills as if they heard the flood rising.

CONSPIRACY

IT is all carefully arranged. Everything is arranged. It is arranged that men should be
broken and that they should be mended. Just
as you send your clothes to the laundry and
mend them when they come back, so we send
our men to the trenches and mend them when
they come back again. You send your socks
and your shirts again and again to the laundry, and you sew up the tears and clip the
ravelled edges again and again just as many
times as they will stand it. And then you
throw them away. And we send our men to
the war again and again, just as long as they
will stand it; just until they are dead, and then
we throw them into the ground.

It is all arranged. Ten kilometres from
here along the road is the place where men
are wounded. This is the place where they
are mended. We have all the things here for

mending, the tables and the needles, and the thread and the knives and the scissors, and many curious things that you never use for your clothes.

We bring our men up along the dusty road where the bushes grow on either side and the green trees. They come by in the mornings in companies, marching with strong legs, with firm steps. They carry their knapsacks easily. Their knapsacks and their guns and their greatcoats are not heavy for them. They wear their caps jauntily, tilted to one side. Their faces are ruddy and their eyes bright. They smile and call out with strong voices. They throw kisses to the girls in the fields.

We send our men up the broken road between bushes of barbed wire and they come back to us, one by one, two by two in ambulances, lying on stretchers. They lie on their backs on the stretchers and are pulled out of the ambulances as loaves of bread are pulled out of the oven. The stretchers slide out of the mouths of the ambulances with the men on them. The men cannot move. They are carried into a shed, unclean bundles, very heavy, covered with brown blankets.

We receive these bundles. We pull off a blanket. We observe that this is a man. He makes feeble whining sounds like an animal. He lies still; he smells bad; he smells like a corpse; he can only move his tongue; he tries to moisten his lips with his tongue.

This is the place where he is to be mended. We lift him on to a table. We peel off his clothes, his coat and his shirt and his trousers and his boots. We handle his clothes that are stiff with blood. We cut off his shirt with large scissors. We stare at the obscene sight of his innocent wounds. He allows us to do this. He is helpless to stop us. We wash off the dry blood round the edges of his wounds. He suffers us to do as we like with him. He says no word except that he is thirsty and we do not give him to drink.

We confer together over his body and he hears us. We discuss his different parts in terms that he does not understand, but he listens while we make calculations with his heart beats and the pumping breath of his lungs.

We conspire against his right to die. We experiment with his bones, his muscles, his sinews, his blood. We dig into the yawning mouths of his wounds. Helpless openings, they let us into the secret places of his body. We plunge deep into his body. We make discoveries within his body. To the shame of the havoc of his limbs we add the insult of our curiosity and the curse of our purpose, the purpose to remake him. We lay odds on his chances of escape, and we combat with death, his Saviour.

It is our business to do this. He knows and he allows us to do it. He finds himself in the operating room. He lays himself out. He bares himself to our knives. His mind is annihilated. He pours out his blood unconscious. His red blood is spilled and pours over the table on to the floor while he sleeps.

After this, while he is still asleep, we carry him into another place and put him to bed. He awakes bewildered as children do, expecting, perhaps, to find himself at home with his mother leaning over him, and he moans a little and then lies still again. He is helpless, so we do for him what he cannot do for himself, and he is grateful. He accepts his helplessness. He is obedient. We feed him, and he eats. We fatten him up, and he allows himself to be fattened. Day after day he lies there and we watch him. All day and all night he is watched. Every day his wounds are uncovered and cleaned, scraped and washed and bound up again. His body does not belong to him. It belongs to us for the moment, not for long He knows why we tend it so carefully. He. knows what we are fattening and cleaning it up for; and while we handle it he smiles.

He is only one among thousands. They are all the same. They all let us do with them what we like. They all smile as if they were grateful. When we hurt them they try not to cry out, not wishing to hurt our feelings. And often they apologise for dying. They would not die and disappoint us if they could help it. Indeed, in their helplessness they do the best they can to help us get them ready to go back again.

It is only ten kilometres up the road, the place where they go to be torn again and mangled. Listen; you can hear how well it works. There is the sound of cannon and the sound of the ambulances bringing the wounded, and the sound of the tramp of strong men going

things. You finger the glass syringes exquisitely and pick up the fine needles easily with slender pincers and with the glass beads poised neatly on your rosy finger tips you saw them with tiny saws. You flaunt your perfect movements in the face of his mysterious exhaustion. You show off the skilled movements of your hands beside the erratic jerkings of his terrible limbs.

Why do you rub his grey flesh with the stained scrap of cotton and stick the needle deep into his side? Why do you do it?

Death is inexorable and the place of death is void. You have crowded the room with all manner of things. Why do you crowd all these things up to the edge of the great emptiness?

You seem to have so much to do. Wait. Wait. A miracle is going to happen. Death is coming into the room. There is no time for all this business. There is only one moment between this man and eternity.

You still fuss about busily. You move your feet and rustle your petticoats. You are continually doing things with your hands. You keep on doing things. Why do you keep on doing things? Death is annoyed at you fussing.

The man's spirit is invisible. Why do you light the lamp? You cannot see the God of Death with your splendid eyes. Does it please you to see the sweat on that forehead and the glaze on the eyeballs?

Hush, you are making a noise. Why do you make a noise? No, as you say, he cannot hear you, but cannot you hear? Eternity is soundless, but hush! Let us listen. Let us listen. Maybe we shall hear the stirring of wings or the sighing tremor of his soul passing.

Ah! What are you doing? Why do you move? You are filling the room with sound as you have filled it with objects. You are annoying death with your ridiculous things and the noise of your foolish business.

What do you say? He is dead? You say he is dead?

And here are all your things, your blankets and your bottles and your basins. The blankets weigh down upon his body. They hang down over the bed. Your syringes and your needles and your uncorked bottles are all about in confusion. You have stained your fingers.

125

There is a spot on your white apron; but you are superb, and here are all your things about you, all your queer things, all the confusion of your precious things.

What have you and all your things to do with the dying of this man? Nothing. Take them away.

IN THE OPERATING ROOM

THE operating room is the section of a wooden shed. Thin partitions separate it from the X-ray room on one side, and the sterilizing room on the other. Another door communicates with a corridor. There are three wounded men on three operating tables. Surgeons, nurses and orderlies are working over them. The doors keep opening and shutting. The boiler is pounding and bubbling in the sterilizing room. There is a noise of steam escaping, of feet hurrying down the corridor, of ambulances rolling past the windows, and behind all this, the rhythmic pounding of the guns bombarding at a distance of ten miles or so.

1st Patient: Mother of God! Mother of God!

2nd Patient: Softly. Softly. You hurt me. Ah! You are hurting me.

3rd Patient: I am thirsty.

127

1st Surgeon: Cut the dressing, Mademoiselle.

2nd Surgeon: What's his ticket say? Show it to me. What's the X-ray show?

3rd Surgeon: Abdomen. Bad pulse. I wonder now?

1st Patient: In the name of God be careful. I suffer. I suffer.

1st Surgeon: At what time were you wounded?

1st Patient : At five this morning.

1st Surgeon: Where?

1st Patient: In the arm.

1st Surgeon: Yes, yes, but in what sector?

1st Patient: In the trenches near Besanghe.

1st Surgeon: Shell or bullet?

1st Patient: Shell. Merciful God, what are you doing?

A nurse comes in from the corridor. Her apron is splashed with blood.

Nurse: There's a lung just come in. Hæmorrhage. Can one of you take him?

1st Surgeon: In a few minutes. In five minutes. Now then, Mademoiselle, strap down that other arm tighter.

Nurse (in doorway) to 2nd Surgeon:

There's a knee for you, doctor, and three elbows. In five minutes I'll send in the lung. (Exit.)

3rd Patient: I'm thirsty. A drink. Give me a drink.

3rd Surgeon: In a little while. You must wait a little.

2nd Patient: Mother of Jesus, not like that. Don't turn my foot like that. Not that way. Take care. Great God, take care! I can't bear it. I tell you, I can't bear it!

2nd Surgeon: There, there, don't excite yourself. You've got a nasty leg, very nasty. Smells bad. Mademoiselle, hold his leg up. It's not pretty at all, this leg.

2nd Patient: Ah, doctor, doctor. What are you doing? Aiee——.

2nd Surgeon: Be quiet. Don't move. Don't touch the wound I tell you. Idiot! Hold his leg. Keep your hands off, you animal. Hold his leg higher. Strap his hands down.

3rd Patient (feebly): I am thirsty. I die of thirst. A drink! A drink!

2nd Patient (screaming): You're killing me. Killing me! I'll die of it! Aieeeee——.

3rd Patient (softly): I am thirsty. For pity a drink.

3rd Surgeon: Have you vomited blood, old man?

3rd Patient: I don't know. A drink please, doctor.

3rd Surgeon: Does it hurt here?

3rd Patient: No, I don't think so. A drink, sister, in pity's name, a drink.

Nurse: I can't give you a drink. It would hurt you. You are wounded in the stomach.

3rd Patient: So thirsty. Just a little drink. Just a drop. Sister for pity, just a drop.

3rd Surgeon: Moisten his lips. How long ago were you wounded?

3rd Patient: I don't know. In the night. Some night.

3rd Surgeon: Last night?

3rd Patient: Perhaps last night. I don't know. I lay in the mud a long time. Please sister a drink. Just a little drink.

1st Patient: What's in that bottle? What are you doing to me?

1st Surgeon: Keep still I tell you.

1st Patient: It burns! It's burning me! No

more. No more! I beg of you, doctor; I can't bear any more!

1st Surgeon: Nonsense. This won't last a minute. There's nothing the matter with you. Your wounds are nothing.

1st Patient: You say it's nothing. My God, what are you doing now? Ai—ee!

1st Surgeon: It's got to be cleaned out. There's a piece of shell, bits of coat, all manner of dirt in it.

2nd Patient: Jeanne, petite Marie, Jean, where are you? Little Jean, where are you?

2nd Surgeon: Your leg is not at all pretty, my friend. We shall have to take it off.

2nd Patient: Oh, my poor wife! I have three children, doctor, If you take my leg off what will become of them and of the farm? Great God, to suffer like this!

2nd Surgeon to 1st Surgeon: Look here a moment. It smells bad. Gangrenous. What do you think?

1st Surgeon: No good waiting.

2nd Surgeon: Well, my friend, will you have it off?

2nd Patient: If you say so, doctor. Oh, my poor wife, my poor Jeanne. What will become of you? The children are too little to work in the fields.

2nd Surgeon (to nurse): Begin with the chloroform. We're going to put you to sleep, old man. Breathe deep. Breathe through the mouth. Is my saw there? Where is my amputating saw? Who's got my saw?

3rd Patient (softly): A drink, a drink. Give me a drink.

3rd Surgeon: I can do nothing with a pulse like that. Give him serum, five hundred c.c.s and camphorated oil and strychnine. Warm him up a bit.

Door opens, nurse enters, followed by two stretcher bearers.

Nurse: Here's the lung. Are you ready for it?

1st Surgeon: In a minute. One minute. Leave him there.

The stretcher bearers put their stretcher on the floor and go out.

2nd Patient: (half under chloroform): Aha! Aha! Ahead there, you son of a ——. Forward! Forward! What a stink! I've got him! Now I've got you. Quick, quick! Let me go! Let me go! Jeannette, quick, quick, Jeannette! I'm coming. Marie? Little Jean, where are you?

2nd Surgeon: Tighten those straps. He's strong, poor devil.

1st Patient: Is it finished?

1st Surgeon: Very nearly. Keep quite still. Now then, the dressings mademoiselle. There you are old man. Don't bandage the arm too tight, mademoiselle. Get him out now. Hi, stretcher bearers, lift up that one from the floor, will you?

3rd Surgeon: It's no use operating. Almost no pulse.

3rd Patient: For pity a drink!

3rd Surgeon: Give him a drink. It won't matter. I can do nothing.

2nd Surgeon: I shall have to amputate above the knee. Is he under?

Nurse: Almost.

3rd Patient: For pity a drink.

Nurse: There, don't lift your head; here is a drink. Drink this.

3rd Patient: It is good. Thank you, sister.

1st Surgeon: Take this man to Ward 3. Now then, mademoiselle, cut the dressings.

3rd Surgeon: I can do nothing here. Send me the next one.

3rd Patient: I cannot see. I cannot see any more. Sister, where are you?

1st Surgeon: How's your spine case of yesterday?

3rd Surgeon: Just what you would expect— paralysed from the waist down.

1st Surgeon: They say the attack is for five in the morning.

3rd Surgeon: Orders are to evacuate every possible bed to-day.

3rd Patient: It is dark. Are you there, sister?

Nurse: Yes, old man, I'm here. Shall I send for a priest, doctor?

3rd Surgeon: Too late. Poor devil. It's hopeless when they come in like that, after lying for hours in the mud. There, it's finished. Call the stretcher bearers.

1st Surgeon: Quick, a basin! God! how the blood spouts. Quick, quick, quick! Three holes in this lung.

2nd Surgeon: Take that leg away, will you? There's no room to move here.

3rd Surgeon: Take this dead man away, and bring the next abdomen. Wipe that table, mademoiselle, while I wash my hands. And you, there, mop up the floor a bit.

The doors open and shut. Stretcher bearers go out and come in. A nurse comes from the sterilizing room with a pile of nickel drums in her arms. Another nurse goes out with trays of knives and other instruments. The nurse from the corridor comes back. An officer appears at the window.

Nurse: Three knees have come in, two more abdomens, five heads.

Officer (through the window): The Médecin Inspecteur will be here in half an hour. The General is coming at two to decorate all amputés.

1st Surgeon: We'll get no lunch to-day, and I'm hungry. There, I call that a very neat amputation.

2nd Surgeon : Three holes stopped in this lung in three minutes by the clock. Pretty quick, eh?

3rd Surgeon: Give me a light, some one. My experience is that if abdomens have to wait more than six hours it's no good. You can't do anything. I hope that chap got the oysters in Amiens! Oysters sound good to me.

BLIND

The door at the end of the baraque kept opening and shutting to let in the stretcher bearers. As soon as it opened a crack the wind scurried in and came hopping toward me across the bodies of the men that covered the floor, nosing under the blankets, lifting the flaps of heavy coats, and burrowing among the loose heaps of clothing and soiled bandages. Then the grizzled head of a stretcher bearer would appear, butting its way in, and he would emerge out of the black storm into the bright fog that seemed to fill the place, dragging the stretcher after him, and then the old one at the other end of the load would follow, and they would come slowly down the centre of the hut looking for a clear place on the floor.

The men were laid out in three rows on either side of the central alley way. It was a big hut, and there were about sixty stretchers in each row. There was space between the heads of one row and the feet of another row, but no space to pass between the stretchers in the same row; they touched. The old territorials who worked with me passed up and down between the heads and feet. I had a squad of thirty of these old orderlies and two sergeants and two priests, who were expert dressers. Wooden screens screened off the end of the hut opposite the entrance. Behind these were the two dressing tables where the priests dressed the wounds of the new arrivals and got them ready for the surgeons, after the old men had undressed them and washed their feet. In one corner was my kitchen where I kept all my syringes and hypodermic needles and stimulants.

It was just before midnight when the stretcher bearers brought in the blind man, and there was no space on the floor anywhere; so they stood waiting, not knowing what to do with him.

I said from the floor in the second row: "Just a minute, old ones. You can put him here in a minute." So they waited with the

blind man suspended in the bright, hot, misty
air between them, like a pair of old horses in
shafts with their heads down, while the little
boy who had been crying for his mother died
with his head on my breast. Perhaps he
thought the arms holding him when he jerked
back and died belonged to some woman I had
never seen, some woman waiting somewhere
for news of him in some village, somewhere in
France. How many women, I wondered, were
waiting out there in the distance for news of
these men who were lying on the floor? But I
stopped thinking about this the minute the
boy was dead. It didn't do to think. I didn't
as a rule, but the boy's very young voice had
startled me. It had come through to me as a
real voice will sound sometimes through a
dream, almost waking you, but now it had
stopped, and the dream was thick round me
again, and I laid him down, covered his face
with the brown blanket, and called two other
old ones.

"Put this one in the corridor to make more
room here," I said; and I saw them lift him
up. When they had taken him away, the
stretcher bearers who had been waiting

brought the blind one and put him down in the cleared space. They had to come round to the end of the front row and down between the row of feet and row of heads; they had to be very careful where they stepped; they had to lower the stretcher cautiously so as not to jostle the men on either side (there was just room), but these paid no attention. None of the men lying packed together on the floor noticed each other in this curious dream-place.

I had watched this out of the corner of my eye, busy with something that was not very like a man. The limbs seemed to be held together only by the strong stuff of the uniform. The head was unrecognisable. It was a monstrous thing, and a dreadful rattling sound came from it. I looked up and saw the chief surgeon standing over me. I don't know how he got there. His small shrunken face was wet and white; his eyes were brilliant and feverish; his incredible hands that saved so many men so exquisitely, so quickly, were in the pockets of his white coat.

"Give him morphine," he said, "a double dose. As much as you like." He pulled a cigarette out of his pocket. "In cases like this, if I am not about, give morphine; enough, you understand." Then he vanished like a ghost. He went back to his operating room, a small white figure with round shoulders, a magician, who performed miracles with knives. He went away through the dream.

I gave the morphine, then crawled over and looked at the blind man's ticket. I did not know, of course, that he was blind until I read his ticket. A large round white helmet covered the top half of his head and face; only his nostrils and mouth and chin were uncovered. The surgeon in the dressing station behind the trenches had written on his ticket, "Shot through the eyes. Blind."

Did he know? I asked myself. No, he couldn't know yet. He would still be wondering, waiting, hoping, down there in that deep, dark silence of his, in his own dark personal world. He didn't know he was blind; no one would have told him. I felt his pulse. It was strong and steady. He was a long, thin man, but his body was not very cold and the pale lower half of his clear-cut face was not very pale. There was something beautiful about him. In his case there was no hurry, no necessity to rush him through to the operating room. There was plenty of time. He would always be blind.

One of the orderlies was going up and down with hot tea in a bucket. I beckoned to him.

I said to the blind one: "Here is a drink." He didn't hear me, so I said it more loudly against the bandage, and helped him lift his head, and held the tin cup to his mouth below the thick edge of the bandage. I did not think then of what was hidden under the bandage. I think of it now. Another head case across the hut had thrown off his blanket and risen from his stretcher. He was standing stark naked except for his head bandage, in the middle of the hut, and was haranguing the crowd in a loud voice with the gestures of a political orator. But the crowd, lying on the floor, paid no attention to him. They did not notice him. I called to Gustave and Pierre to go to him.

The blind man said to me: "Thank you, sister, you are very kind. That is good. I thank you." He had a beautiful voice. I noticed the great courtesy of his speech. But they were all courteous. Their courtesy when they died, their reluctance to cause me any trouble by dying or suffering, was one of the things it didn't do to think about.

Then I left him, and presently forgot that he was there waiting in the second row of stretchers on the left side of the long crowded floor.

Gustave and Pierre had got the naked orator back on to his stretcher and were wrapping him up again in his blankets. I let them deal with him and went back to my kitchen at the other end of the hut, where my syringes and hypodermic needles were boiling in saucepans. I had received by post that same morning a dozen beautiful new platinum needles. I was very pleased with them. I said to one of the dressers as I fixed a needle on my syringe and held it up, squirting the liquid through it; "Look. I've some lovely new needles." He said: "Come and help me a moment. Just cut this bandage, please." I went over to his dressing-table. He darted off to a voice that was shrieking somewhere. There was a man stretched on the table. His brain came off in my hands when I lifted the bandage from his head.

When the dresser came back I said: "His brain came off on the bandage."

"Where have you put it?"

"I put it in the pail under the table."

"It's only one half of his brain," he said, looking into the man's skull. "The rest is here."

I left him to finish the dressing and went about my own business. I had much to do.

It was my business to sort out the wounded as they were brought in from the ambulances and to keep them from dying before they got to the operating rooms : it was my business to sort out the nearly dying from the dying. I was there to sort them out and tell how fast life was ebbing in them. Life was leaking away from all of them; but with some there was no hurry, with others it was a case of minutes. It was my business to create a counter-wave of life, to create the flow against the ebb. It was like a tug of war with the tide. The ebb of life was cold. When life was ebbing the man was cold; when it began to flow back, he grew warm. It was all, you see, like a dream. The dying men on the floor were drowned men cast up on the beach, and there was the ebb of life pouring away over them, sucking them away, an invisible tide; and my old orderlies, like old sea-salts out of a lifeboat, were working to save them. I had to watch, to see if they were slipping, being dragged away. If a man were slipping quickly, being sucked down rapidly, I sent runners to the operating rooms. There were six operating rooms on either side of my hut. Medical students in white coats hurried back and forth along the covered corridors between us. It was my business to know which of the wounded could wait and which could not. I had to decide for myself. There was no one to tell me. If I made any mistakes, some would die on their stretchers on the floor under my eyes who need not have died. I didn't worry. I didn't think. I was too busy, too absorbed in what I was doing. I had to judge from what was written on their tickets and from the way they looked and the way they felt to my hand. My hand could tell of itself one kind of cold from another. They were all half-frozen when they arrived, but the chill of their icy flesh wasn't the same as the cold inside them when life was almost ebbed away. My hands could instantly tell the difference between the cold of the harsh bitter night and the stealthy cold of death. Then there was another thing, a small fluttering thing. I didn't think about it or count it. My fingers felt it. I was in a dream, led this way and that by my cute eyes and hands that did many things, and seemed to know what to do.

Sometimes there was no time to read the ticket or touch the pulse. The door kept opening and shutting to let in the stretcher-bearers whatever I was doing. I could not watch when I was giving piqures; but, standing by my table filling a syringe, I could look down over the rough forms that covered the floor and pick out at a distance this one and that one. I had been doing this for two years, and had learned to read the signs. I could tell from the way they twitched, from the peculiar shade of a pallid face, from the look of tight pinched-in nostrils, and in other ways which I could not have explained, that this or that one was slipping over the edge of the beach of life. Then I would go quickly with my long saline needles, or short thick camphor oil needles, and send one of the old ones hurrying along the corridor to the operating rooms. But sometimes there was no need to hurry; sometimes I was too late; with some there was no longer any question of the ebb and flow of life and death; there was nothing to do.

The hospital throbbed and hummed that night like a dynamo. The operating rooms were ablaze; twelve surgical équipes were at work; boilers steamed and whistled; nurses hurried in and out of the sterilizing rooms carrying big shining metal boxes and ena-melled trays; feet were running, slower feet shuffling. The hospital was going full steam ahead. I had a sense of great power, ex-hilaration and excitement. A loud wind was howling. It was throwing itself like a pack of wolves against the flimsy wooden walls, and the guns were growling. Their voices were dying away. I thought of them as a pack of beaten dogs, slinking away across the dark waste where the dead were lying and the wounded who had not yet been picked up, their only cover the windy blanket of the bitter November night.

And I was happy. It seemed to me that the crazy crowded bright hot shelter was a beautiful place. I thought, "This is the second battlefield. The battle now is going on over the helpless bodies of these men. It is we who are doing the fighting now, with their real enemies." And I thought of the chief surgeon, the wizard working like lightning through the night, and all the others wielding their flashing knives against the invisible enemy. The wounded had begun to arrive at noon. It was now past midnight, and the door kept opening and shutting to let in the stretcher-bearers, and the ambulances kept lurching in at the gate. Lanterns were moving through the windy dark from shed to shed. The nurses were out there in the scattered huts, putting the men to bed when they came over the dark ground, asleep, from the operating rooms. They would wake up in clean warm beds—those who did wake up.

"We will send you the dying, the desperate, the moribund," the Inspector-General had said. "You must expect a thirty per cent. mortality." So we had got ready for it; we had organised to dispute that figure.

We had built brick ovens, four of them, down the centre of the hut, and on top of these, galvanised iron cauldrons of boiling water were steaming. We had driven nails all the way down the wooden posts that held up the roof and festooned the posts with red rubber hot-water bottles. In the corner near to my kitchen we had partitioned off a cubicle, where we built a light bed, a rough wooden frame lined with electric light bulbs, where a man could be cooked back to life again. My own kitchen was an arrangement of shelves for saucepans and syringes and needles of different sizes, and cardboard boxes full of ampoules of camphor oil and strychnine and caffeine and morphine, and large ampoules of sterilized salt and water, and dozens of beautiful sharp shining needles were always on the boil.

It wasn't much to look at, this reception hut. It was about as attractive as a goods yard in a railway station, but we were very proud of it, my old ones and I. We had got it ready, and it was good enough for us. We could revive the cold dead there; snatch back the men who were slipping over the edge; hoist them out of the dark abyss into life again. And because our mortality at the end of three months was only nineteen per cent., not thirty, well it was the most beautiful place in the world to me and my old grizzled Pépères, Gaston and Pierre and Leroux and the others were to me like shining archangels. But I didn't think about this. I think of it now. I only knew it then, and was happy. Yes, I was happy there.

Looking back, I do not understand that woman—myself—standing in that confused goods yard filled with bundles of broken human flesh. The place by one o'clock in the morning was a shambles. The air was thick with steaming sweat, with the effluvia of mud, dirt, blood. The men lay in their stiff uniforms that were caked with mud and dried blood, their great boots on their feet; stained bandages showing where a trouser leg or a sleeve had been cut away. Their faces gleamed faintly, with a faint phosphorescence. Some who could not breathe lying down were propped up on their stretchers against the wall, but most were prone on their backs, staring at the steep iron roof.

The old orderlies moved from one stretcher

to another, carefully, among the piles of clothing,
boots and blood-soaked bandages—careful not
to step on a hand or a sprawling twisted foot.
They carried zinc pails of hot water and slabs
of yellow soap and scrubbing brushes. They
gathered up the heaps of clothing, and made
little bundles of the small things out of
pockets, or knelt humbly, washing the big
yellow stinking feet that protruded from
under the brown blankets. It was the business of these old ones to undress the wounded,
wash them, wrap them in blankets, and put
hot-water bottles at their feet and sides. It
was a difficult business peeling the stiff uniform from a man whose hip or shoulder was
fractured, but the old ones were careful.
Their big peasant hands were gentle—
very, very gentle and careful. They handled
the wounded men as if they were children.
Now, looking back, I see their rough power-
ful visages, their shaggy eye-brows, their big
clumsy, gentle hands. I see them go down
on their stiff knees; I hear their shuffling feet
and their soft gruff voices answering the
voices of the wounded, who are calling to
them for drinks, or to God for mercy.

The old ones had orders from the commandant not to cut the good cloth of the uniforms if they could help it, but they had orders from me not to hurt the men, and they obeyed me. They slit up the heavy trousers and slashed across the stiff tunics with long scissors, and pulled very slowly, very carefully at the heavy boots, and the wounded men did not groan or cry out very much. They were mostly very quiet. When they did cry out they usually apologised for the annoyance of their agony. Only now and then a wind of pain would sweep over the floor, tossing the legs and arms, then subside again.

I think that woman, myself, must have been in a trance, or under some horrid spell. Her feet are lumps of fire, her face is clammy, her apron is splashed with blood; but she moves ceaselessly about with bright burning eyes and handles the dreadful wreckage of men as if in a dream. She does not seem to notice the wounds or the blood. Her eyes seem to be watching something that comes and goes and darts in and out among the prone bodies. Her eyes and her hands and her ears are alert, in-

tent on the unseen thing that scurries and
hides and jumps out of the corner on to the
face of a man when she's not looking. But
quick, something makes her turn. Quick, she
is over there, on her knees fighting the thing
off, driving it away, and now it's got another
victim. It's like a dreadful game of hide and
seek among the wounded. All her faculties are
intent on it. The other things that are going
on, she deals with automatically.

There is a constant coming and going.
Medical students run in and out.

"What have you got ready?"

"I've got three knees, two spines, five abdomens, twelve heads. Here's a lung case—
hæmorrhage. He can't wait." She is binding
the man's chest; she doesn't look up.

"Send him along."

"Pierre! Gaston! Call the stretcher-
bearers to take the lung to Monsieur D——."
She fastens the tight bandage, tucks the
blanket quickly round the thin shoulders. The
old men lift him. She hurries back to her
saucepans to get a new needle.

A surgeon appears.

"Where's that knee of mine? I left it in the

saucepan on the window ledge. I had boiled
it up for an experiment."

"One of the orderlies must have taken it,"
she says, putting her old needle on to boil.

"Good God ! Did he mistake it?"

"Jean, did you take a saucepan you found
on the windowsill?"

"Yes, sister, I took it. I thought it was for
the casse croûte ; it looked like a ragout of
mouton. I have it here."

"Well, it was lucky he didn't eat it. It was
a knee I had cut out, you know."

It is time for the old ones "casse croûte."
It is after one o'clock. At one o'clock the
orderlies have cups of coffee and chunks of
bread and meat. They eat their supper
gathered round the stoves where the iron
cauldrons are boiling. The surgeons and the
sisters attached to the operating rooms are
drinking coffee too in the sterilizing rooms.
I do not want any supper. I am not hungry.
I am not tired. I am busy. My eyes are busy
and my fingers. I am conscious of nothing
about myself but my eyes, hands and feet.
My feet are a nuisance, they are swollen,
hurting lumps, but my fingers are perfectly

153

one body, suffering and bleeding. It is a kind of bliss to me to feel this. I am a little delirious, but my head is cool enough, it seems to me.

"No, not that one. He can wait. Take the next one to Monsieur D——, and this one to Monsieur Guy, and this one to Monsieur Robert. We will put this one on the electric light bed ; he has no pulse. More hot-water bottles here, Gaston.

"Do you feel cold, mon vieux?"

"Yes, I think so, but pray do not trouble."

I go with him into the little cubicle, turn on the light bulbs, leave him to cook there; and as I come out again to face the strange heaving dream, I suddenly hear a voice calling me, a new far-away hollow voice.

"Sister! My sister ! Where are you?"

I am startled. It sounds so far away, so hollow and so sweet. It sounds like a bell high up in the mountains. I do not know where it comes from. I look down over the rows of men lying on their backs, one close to the other, packed together on the floor, and I cannot tell where the voice comes from. Then I hear it again.

156

"Sister! Oh, my sister, where are you?"

A lost voice. The voice of a lost man, wandering in the mountains, in the night. It is the blind man calling. I had forgotten him. I had forgotten that he was there. He could wait. The others could not wait. So I had left him and forgotten him.

Something in his voice made me run, made my heart miss a beat. I ran down the centre alley way, round and up again, between the two rows, quickly, carefully stepping across to him over the stretchers that separated us. He was in the second row. I could just squeeze through to him.

"I am coming," I called to him. "I am coming."

I knelt beside him. "I am here," I said; but he lay quite still on his back; he didn't move at all; he hadn't heard me. So I took his hand and put my mouth close to his bandaged head and called to him with desperate entreaty.

"I am here. What is it? What is the matter?"

He didn't move even then, but he gave a long shuddering sigh of relief.

"I thought I had been abandoned here, all alone," he said softly in his far-away voice.

I seemed to awake then. I looked round me and began to tremble, as one would tremble if one awoke with one's head over the edge of a precipice. I saw the wounded packed round us, hemming us in. I saw his comrades, thick round him, and the old ones shuffling about, working and munching their hunks of bread, and the door opening to let in the stretcher bearers. The light poured down on the rows of faces. They gleamed faintly. Four hundred faces were staring up at the roof, side by side. The blind man didn't know. He thought he was alone, out in the dark. That was the precipice, that reality.

"You are not alone," I lied. "There are many of your comrades here, and I am here, and there are doctors and nurses. You are with friends here, not alone."

"I thought," he murmured in that far-away voice, "that you had gone away and forgotten me, and that I was abandoned here alone."

My body rattled and jerked like a machine

out of order. I was awake now, and I seemed to be breaking to pieces.

"No," I managed to lie again. "I had not forgotten you, nor left you alone." And I looked down again at the visible half of his face and saw that his lips were smiling.

At that I fled from him. I ran down the long, dreadful hut and hid behind my screen and cowered, sobbing, in a corner, hiding my face.

The old ones were very troubled. They didn't know what to do. Presently I heard them whispering:

"She is tired," one said.

"Yes, she is tired."

"She should go off to bed," another said.

"We will manage somehow without her," they said.

Then one of them timidly stuck a grizzled head round the corner of the screen. He held his tin cup in his hands. It was full of hot coffee. He held it out, offering it to me. He didn't know of anything else that he could do for me.

THE General came one morning after the big attack, to visit the hospital. He went through all the huts, stopping beside each bed to speak to the wounded, and he decorated every man who had lost a leg or an arm with the Medaille Militaire. It was a short ceremony. The General stood at the foot of the bed and recited quickly the military formula citing the man for bravery in the field, and he raised his sword and saluted the wounded man; then he pinned the medal on his nightshirt, and, leaning over him, kissed him on both cheeks. When he rose and moved on down the ward, "the amputé" found an envelope on his coverlet with a hundred francs in it. The General, so they said, gave all his pay to the men in this way.

He admired the white coverlets with their gay patterns of pink or red flowers. He had a stony face and his eyes were like bits of blue steel; but he congratulated us on the gay appearance of our huts. He said, looking out of the door at the bare ground, the ugly sheds, and the artillery rattling down the road past the flimsy gate of the hospital, that to awake after a battle in a clean bed, dressed in a pink nightshirt and with a white coverlet with pink roses on it spread over your feet, must be like waking in Paradise.

I said, following him from bed to bed, that the coverlets came from Selfridges and cost two shillings apiece, and I thought they were worth it. They even, I said, made the difference sometimes between a man's slipping away or back into the world when he awoke.

The General did not have very much time. All the beds were full. He couldn't stop to talk to each man for more than half a minute, but when he came to No. 11 in Mademoiselle de M——'s ward and saw the ugly, scarred, black, burnt-up face grinning on the pillow and the eyes twinkling so astonishingly under the singed eyebrows, he seemed very taken aback.

"What's the matter with his face?" he

asked me in a low tone. "It's a cinder! Why is he so jolly?"

"The shell burst so near that he was burnt. All his skin is burnt black, you see. Both arms are broken, and both legs. He is wounded all over his body. God knows why he is so jolly."

There was very little to be seen of the man but his merry, burnt, scarred face. The cradle over his broken legs hid him from view till you got round it close to his pillow. His arms were in splints, and were supported by pulleys attached to a scaffolding over his bed. He couldn't move any part of himself but his head. He grinned up at us and began to talk in his rough patois that was very difficult to understand. He was a great talker, was No. 11. He must have been the wag of his village. He came from somewhere near Nantes. He had a very strong accent and a rough rollicking comical voice that bubbled out of him in a stream in answer to the General's enquiry as to how he felt.

The General listened, fascinated and puzzled. "What does he say?" he asked me.

"He says he feels fine, except for his legs

and arms. He says he's in fine shape. He says if he hadn't had to wait on the battlefield for four days and nights his wounds would be nothing. He was lost, he said, in No Man's Land, and had to crawl along on his stomach, and it was a slow business because his legs and arms were broken. He hitched himself along somehow on his stomach, but it was a slow way of travelling. He says he had to lie quiet in the daytime, and could only crawl along at night, and he didn't know which way to make for. He said the men were lying out there as thick as flies, but the stretcher-bearers didn't come his way, so he is lucky to be here. He says he's always lucky, always has been."

The bright laughing eyes in the burnt-up face watched me while I explained. When I paused he began to talk again.

"What's he saying now?" asked the General. "He seems to think it is all a good joke."

"He says when he woke up here and saw the pink roses on his bedspread he thought he was in Heaven, and then he felt a great hunger, and knew he was alive, and that his luck was good; a miracle had happened. He says the priest at home told him about miracles, and he always poked fun at him."

The General was evidently intrigued, but he hadn't much time. "Four days and four nights out there! I congratulate you, mon vieux." He turned reluctantly to go.

"One minute, mon General, one minute. I saw something, a little thing. I would like to tell you what I saw out there on the battle-field."

The General turned, came back again past the mountain of bedclothes and looked down with his steel-blue eyes into the ugly black-ened face. "Tell me," he said, "what did you see?" The General might possibly have looked in that way at a beautiful woman whom he loved very tenderly in the secret depths of his stone heart. His eyes were fixed intently, questioningly, wistfully, on the ugly visage with its incredible jollity. "What was it you saw, mon vieux, quick—tell me."

"It was like this. There were men dying out there and there were priests on their knees going from one to the other. It was early morning, just after sunrise, and the Boche were shelling again. Every now and

then a shell would fall and a shower of shrapnel, and pht—some poor devil would stop
groaning. I wasn't dying, you see, so I didn't
call to the priests. I'd been crawling along
in the dark during the night, but now in the
light I lay still, pretending I was dead,
because of the sniping. There was a man
dying a little way off, and a priest was kneeling, holding up a crucifix in front of him, and
a little further off there was another man
dying, who was a Jew, and the Rabbi of his
regiment was kneeling beside him; and just
then, when I watched, I saw the priest fall
forward on the ground, on his face, with the
crucifix in his hands. The Rabbi saw it, too.
His man was just dead, and he saw that the
priest had been hit in the back. He looked
over his shoulder, you see, when the shell
exploded. Then he crawled over on his hands
and knees to where the priest was lying and
took the crucifix out of his hands and knelt
just where the priest had been kneeling, and
held up the crucifix in front of the eyes of the
man, the good Catholic who was dying; and
he didn't know the difference, you see; and
so he died, not noticing the priest was dead

and the Rabbi was in his place—only seeing the crucifix."

There was a silence. The General drew himself up and turned away, staring out of the window. Two stretcher-bearers were passing, carrying a tightly rolled bundle to the morgue. I did not try to see the General's face. The man in the bed was smiling.

"Lucky for him, wasn't it?" he said to me. "I'll tell the priest in my village when I get home, and I'll tell him about the coverlet with the pink roses. Maybe the wife could get one like it."

"They come from Selfridges," I said. "They cost five francs. I'll send you one when the war is over."

THEY were very big men. They must have stood six feet three or four in their socks, but, of course, I never saw them standing up. I only saw them horizontal, carried in on stretchers, flat on their backs. One of them I saw next morning in his bed, the other one I only saw on his stretcher in the receiving hut. He was carried away, was never put into a bed. I knew I would never see him again. His pal knew it, too.

It was a mistake their coming to us. The English were co-operating with the French in the attack, and these two had been picked up in the confusion by a French ambulance. I remember how surprised I was when I saw the khaki uniforms. It was the same night that the blind man came in, or, to be exact, it was toward morning of the same day.

The hut was still crowded with wounded.

The door still kept opening and shutting to let in the stretcher-bearers. We seemed to be making no headway. The men came in as fast as we could despatch them to the operating rooms. Would there never be an end to it? Would the sound of the ambulances lurching in at the gate never stop? What, I asked myself, was the toll of this last failure to break the German line? How many men had passed through my hands during the last thirty-six hours? I did not know. I had not tried to count them. They were carried in and carried out, and they were always there—the same ones, it seemed to me—suffering the same pain, with the same wounds gaping, the same blood pouring out of them. Cold—they were all so cold—half frozen—and we warmed them, thawed them back to life; and yet there they were, still so cold, still wrapped in cold death; and the dying were still dying, and they were all so courteous about it. They all spoke with such courteous voices, using such beautiful phrases, as if they were in my drawing-room. They apologised gravely in their exhaustion for the dirt, the blood, the ugly wounds.

"Do not trouble, sister. Do not give yourself so much trouble, I beg of you."

"I am sorry, Madame, my bandage is leaking. I would not trouble you, but I think I am bleeding."

"I beg your pardon. No, it is not too bad; no, not unbearable. I didn't mean to do that. A thousand pardons. It is nothing. Yes, I am comfortable now—quite comfortable. Do not trouble yourself in the least, Madame."

Most of them were peasants. The French, I realised, were a nation of peasants. But how was it that, even in their agony, they spoke so beautifully, had such perfect manners, chose such pleasant words; and even when they lay there waiting hour after hour, getting weaker and weaker, that their small thin dying voices, scarcely more than whispers, still kept that note of elegance?

"Yes, I am a little tired, Madame, but it is of no consequence, I assure you."

"That I should die while I wait here is a mere trifle that you must not allow to disturb you," was what they seemed to be saying to me.

I was so accustomed to this elegance of

mind among my poilus that I no longer noticed it. I took it for granted. I did not think about it until the two British Gunners came in. Then suddenly I realised that there are two types of courage, the British and the French, as there are two types of men.

The Gunners were pals. They lay side by side staring at the roof. If they were pleasantly surprised to find an English nurse in this barn of a place, they gave no sign of it. Even the red-faced one, who sat up leaning on his elbow when I approached, took me for granted. The other one lay motionless; his face was grey and damp. Neither of them spoke while I looked at their tickets. The red-faced giant was wounded in the leg, otherwise there was nothing wrong with him; the other was wounded in the abdomen; it was clear that there was no hope for him. I would send him through at once to Rouviere. He would save him if he could be saved, but I knew it was useless. I knelt beside him, looking at his ticket. His name was written on it, and the name of his regiment. I do not remember his name, but he came from somewhere in Lancashire. I was wondering whether I should ask him his address and offer to write to his family. Something in my attitude as I knelt there seemed to strike him. He turned his head ever so slightly toward me, and asked, "Is it serious, sister?"

"Yes, I answered, "it is serious. You are wounded in the stomach. That is always very serious."

For a moment he stared into my eyes, then he turned his head away again, shutting me out. I was dismissed, he had nothing to say to me. I rose to my feet and looked from one to the other. But just as I was moving away, the dying one turned his head again and looked across at his pal. There was a dumb interchange of some sort between them, then the red giant spoke.

"Stick it," he said. That was all he said. They didn't talk any more; they had nothing more to say to each other. A few minutes later the stretcher-bearers carried the Gunner, who was wounded in the abdomen, away to the operating room. He died under the anæsthetic. His pal didn't see him again. I don't know where they took him or where he was buried or where his home was. The other Gunner didn't tell me. He didn't ask me anything about his friend.

I found him the next day in one of the wards sitting up in bed eating his dinner. He didn't say anything when he saw me. He looked very fit and very big, and he seemed to have a good appetite. There was no expression of any kind on his face.

"I said, "Good morning. How are you?"

He answered something. I couldn't understand what he said, so I asked him again, saying, "I didn't quite catch what you said."

"A1 at Lloyd's, Madam," he repeated. That was what he had said.

They were the only two wounded Tommies that passed through my hands during the four years of the war, and that was all that they said to me. I don't know any more about them. The big red one was taken to the British evacuating station that afternoon in an ambulance. There was nothing much the matter with him. He didn't say good-bye. I didn't see him when he left. I remember the only two phrases I heard him utter, one to his pal and one to me :

"Stick it."

"A1 at Lloyd's, Madam."

POEMS

THE HILL

From the top of the hill I looked down on
the beautiful, the gorgeous, the super-
human and monstrous landscape of the
superb exulting war.

There were no trees anywhere, nor any
grasses or green thickets, nor any birds
singing, nor any whisper or flutter of any
little busy creatures.

There was no shelter for field mice or rabbits,
squirrels or men.

The earth was naked and on its naked body
crawled things of iron.

It was evening. The long valley was bathed
in blue shadow and through the shadow, as
if swimming, I saw the iron armies moving.

And iron rivers poured through the wilderness
that was peopled with a phantom iron host.

Lights gleamed down there, a thousand
machine eyes winked.

The sun was setting, gilding the smooth crests of the surging hills. The red tents clustering on their naked yellow sides were like scarlet flowers burning in a shining desert of hills.

Against the sunset, along the sharp edge of a hill, a strange regiment was moving in single file, a regiment of monsters.

They moved slowly along on their stomachs, Dragging themselves forward by their ears.

Their great encircling ears moved round and round like wheels.

They were big and very heavy and heavily armoured.

Obscene crabs, armoured toads, big as houses, They moved slowly forward, crushing under their bellies whatever stood in their way.

A flock of aeroplanes was flying home, a flight of wild ducks with iron wings.

They passed over the monstrous regiment with a roar and disappeared.

I looked down, searching for a familiar thing, a leaf, a tuft of grass, a caterpillar; but the ground dropped away in darkness before my feet, that were planted on a heap of stones.

A path, the old deserted way of cattle, showed below beyond the gaping caverns of abandoned dug-outs, where men had once lived underground. And along the path a German prisoner was stumbling, driven by a black man on a horse.

The black man wore a turban, and he drove the prisoner before him as one drives an animal to market.

These three—the prisoner, the black man and the horse—seemed to have wandered into the landscape by mistake. They were the only creatures of their kind anywhere.

Where had they come from and where were they going in that wilderness of iron with night falling?

The German stumbled on heavily beneath the nose of his captor's horse. I could see the pallid disc of his face thrust forward, and the exhausted lurching of his clumsy body.

He did not look to the right or left, but watching him I saw him trip over a battered iron helmet and an old boot that lay in his way.

Two wooden crosses showed just ahead of him, sticking out of the rough ground.

The three passed in silence.

They passed like ghosts into the deepening shadow of the valley, where the panorama of invisible phantom armies moved, as if swimming.

And as I watched I heard the faint music of bagpipes, and thought that I heard the sound of invisible men marching.

The crests of the naked hills were still touched with gold.

Above the winking eyes of the prodigious war the fragile crescent of the moon floated serene in the perfect sky.

THE SONG OF THE MUD

This is the song of the mud,
The pale yellow glistening mud that covers
the hills like satin;
The grey gleaming silvery mud that is spread
like enamel over the valleys;
The frothing, squirting, spurting, liquid mud
that gurgles along the road beds;
The thick elastic mud that is kneaded and
pounded and squeezed under the hoofs of
the horses;
The invincible, inexhaustible mud of the war
zone.

This is the song of the mud, the uniform of
the poilu.
His coat is of mud, his great dragging flapping
coat, that is too big for him and too heavy;
His coat that once was blue and now is grey
and stiff with the mud that cakes to it.

This is the mud that clothes him.
His trousers and boots are of mud,
And his skin is of mud;
And there is mud in his beard.
His head is crowned with a helmet of mud.
He wears it well.
He wears it as a king wears the ermine that
    bores him.
He has set a new style in clothing;
He has introduced the chic of mud.

This is the song of the mud that wriggles its
    way into battle.
The impertinent, the intrusive, the ubiqui-
    tous, the unwelcome,
The slimy inveterate nuisance,
That fills the trenches,
That mixes in with the food of the soldiers,
That spoils the working of motors and crawls
    into their secret parts,
That spreads itself over the guns,
That sucks the guns down and holds them
    fast in its slimy voluminous lips,
That has no respect for destruction and
    muzzles the bursting shells;
And slowly, softly, easily,

Soaks up the fire, the noise; soaks up the
　　energy and the courage;
Soaks up the power of armies;
Soaks up the battle.
Just soaks it up and thus stops it.

This is the hymn of mud—the obscene, the
　　filthy, the putrid,
The vast liquid grave of our armies.
It has drowned our men.
Its monstrous distended belly reeks with the
　　undigested dead.
Our men have gone into it, sinking slowly,
　　and struggling and slowly disappearing.
Our fine men, our brave, strong, young men;
Our glowing red, shouting, brawny men.
Slowly, inch by inch, they have gone down
　　into it,
Into its darkness, its thickness, its silence.
Slowly, irresistibly, it drew them down,
　　sucked them down,
And they were drowned in thick, bitter,
　　heaving mud.
Now it hides them, Oh, so many of them !
Under its smooth glistening surface it is
　　hiding them blandly.

There is not a trace of them.
There is no mark where they went down.
The mute enormous mouth of the mud has
closed over them.

This is the song of the mud,
The beautiful glistening golden mud that
covers the hills like satin;
The mysterious gleaming silvery mud that is
spread like enamel over the valleys.
Mud, the disguise of the war zone;
Mud, the mantle of battles;
Mud, the smooth fluid grave of our soldiers :
This is the song of the mud.

WHERE IS JEHOVAH?

WHERE is Jehovah the God of Israel with his
   ark and his tabernacle and his pillar of fire?
Here is a people pouring through a wilder-
   ness;
Here are armies camping in a desert ;
Their little tents are like sheep flocking over
   the prairie,
Through a storm of iron, rain and thunder
   and wind of iron.
And pillars of cloud and pillars of fire stand
   all about the quaking earth ;
And a sacrifice is prepared.
Send for Moses, send messengers to Daniel,
   Elijah, Joshua, Gideon—to someone who
   knows where Jehovah is hiding.
Tell them He's wanted—the Great God, the
   Jealous God, the God of Wrath who
   drowned the sinful world of men and sent
   the seven plagues on Egypt, and led His

wilderness to warn or to comfort these
people.

They must look after themselves.

All the host of them, each one of them, quite
alone each one of them, every one of the
hundred thousand of them, alone, must
stand up to meet the war.

With the sky cracking,

With creatures of wide metal wings tearing
the sky over his head,

With the earth shaking,

With the solid earth under his feet giving way,

With the hills on fire and the valleys smoking,
and the few bare trees spitting bullets; and
the long roads like liquid iron torrents,
rolling down on him with guns and iron
food for guns—always guns and more guns
—with these long roads rolling down like
cataracts, to crush him and no way of escape,

With the few houses broken open—no sides,
no covers to them, no protection anywhere,

With all of the universe coming down on him,
the cold dark storm of death coming full
on him,

With the men near him going mad, jibbering,
sobbing, twisting,

With his comrade lying dead under his feet,
With the enemy beyond there—unseen, mysterious,
With eternity waiting, the great silence and
emptiness waiting beyond the noise of the
cannon,
With the memory of his home haunting him
and the face of a woman expectant,
With the soft echoes of his children's laughter
sounding, and shells bursting with roars to
left and right of him, in front and
behind him, but not drowning those small
voices :
He stands there, he keeps on standing; he
stands solid, this sheep man.

He is so small, so quiet in the iron storm.
Why does he stand there? What keeps him
standing there?
Is he not a lost sheep? Why does he not turn,
run, rush, scramble back through the rain,
wind and thunder of iron, bleating with
terror?
Why does he wait to die, and die so quietly,
so humbly, with hope still looking back
from his eyes?

She has been betrayed.
God has betrayed her.
Oh, the pity !
Oh, the terrible, desperate creature !
She believed in God,
And her people worshipped her,
And because she was the Mother of Compassion,
She stood between them and the anger of God.
For she believed in the love of God.
Lifted up above the city,
Above the little dark homes of her helpless people,
She stood, holding up her child to God.
So for centuries she stood lifted up in her humility and love;
And because God had chosen her and given her a child,
Because she had borne a son to Him,
She believed he would be kind to her people.

One day destruction came like roaring dragons out of Heaven, and fell upon the town.
Out of the soft mysterious distance invisible monsters came shrieking past her head.

Flocks of them, unseen, with whistling wings,
    thick as vultures to a carcase in a desert,
They swooped down and sprang upon the city.
And the city writhed in their clutches.
Houses staggered, the streets cracked open.
Meek, motionless, holding her child up to
    Heaven, the Virgin watched from her tower.
She watched the houses vomit,
Watched them reel like drunkards—fall;
Watched the people running, pouring through
    the quaking streets with their treasures
    piled on wagons;
Watched the wagons smothered, buried, with
    the horses, the beds and bedding, the fowls
    and pretty birds in cages.
She could hear the women and the children
    screaming;
And the squealing of horses and groaning of
    cattle and squeaking of pigs caught in burn-
    ing stables, sheds, yards.
Helpless, high above them, prisoner in the
    thundering sky,
Bound to her shaking pedestal, with the
    church walls giving way beneath her,
She stood holding her child up to God, while
    her people screamed to her to save them.

like some old battered image of a faith forgotten by its God.
Note his naked neck and jutting jaw under
the iron hat that's jammed upon his
head;
See how he rounds his shoulders, bends his
back inside his clumsy coat;
And how he leans ahead, gripping with grimy
fists
The muzzle of his gun that digs it butt-end
down into the mud between the solid
columns of his legs.

Look close, come close, pale ghosts !
Come back out of the dim unfinished past;
Crowd up across the edges of the earth,
Where the horizon, like a red hot wire, twists
underneath tremendous smoking blows.
Come up, come up across the quaking ground
that gapes in sudden holes beneath your
feet;
Come fearlessly across the twisting field
where bones of men stick through the tor-
tured mud.
Ghosts have no need to fear.
Look close at this man. Look !

He waits for death;
He watches it approach;
His little bloodshot eyes can see it bearing
down on every side;
He feels it coming underneath his feet, run-
ning, burrowing underneath the ground;
He hears it screaming in the frantic air.
Death that tears the shrieking sky in two,
That suddenly explodes out of the festering
bowels of the earth—
Dreadful and horrid death.
He takes the impact of it on his back, his
chest, his belly and his arms;
Spreads his legs upon its lurching form;
Plants his feet upon its face and breathes deep
into his pumping lungs the gassy breath of
death.
He does not move.
In all the running landscape there's a solitary
thing that's motionless:
The figure of this man.

The sky long since has fallen from its dome.
Terror let loose like a gigantic wind has torn
it from the ceiling of the world,
And it is flapping down in frantic shreds.

The earth ages ago leaped screaming up out
    of the fastness of its ancient laws.
There is no centre now to hold it down.
It rolls and writhes, a shifting tortured thing,
    a floating mass of matter set adrift.
And in between the fluttering tatters of the
    ruined sky,
And the convulsions of the maddened earth,
The man stands solid.
Something holds him there.

What holds him, timid ghosts?
What do you say, you shocked and shuddering
    ghosts,
Dragged from your sheltered vaults;
You who once died in quiet lamp-lit rooms;
Who were companioned to the end by friends;
And closed your eyes in languor on a world
That you had fashioned for your pleasant
    selves?
You scorned this man.
He was for you an ordinary man.
Some of you pitied him, prayed over his soul,
    worried him with stories of Heaven and Hell.
Promised him Heaven if he would be ashamed
    of being what he was,

And everlasting sorrow if he died as he had
    lived, an ordinary man.
You gave him Gods he could not know, and
    images of God; laws he could not keep, and
    punishment.
You were afraid of him.
Everything about him that was his very own
Made you afraid of him.
His love of women, food and drink, and fun,
His clumsy reach for life, his open grabbing fist,
His stupid open gaping heart and mouth.
He was a hungry man,
And you were afraid of him.
None of you trusted him;
No one of you was his friend.

Look at him now. Look well, look long.
Your hungry brute, your ordinary man;
Your fornicator, drunkard, anarchist;
Your ruthless rough seed-sowing male;
Your angry greedy egotist;
Your lost, bewildered, childish dunce;
Come close and look into his haggard face.
It is too late to do him justice now, or even
    speak to him.
But look.

Look at the stillness of his face.
It's made of little fragile bones and flesh,
    tissued of quivering muscles fine as silk;
Exquisite nerves, soft membrane warm with
    blood,
That travels smoothly through the tender
    veins.
One blow, one minute more, and that man's
    face will be a mass of matter, horrid slime
    and little brittle splinters.
He knows.
He waits.
His face remains quite still.
And underneath the bullet-spattered helmet
    on his head
His steady eyes look out.
What is it that looks out?
What is deep mirrored in those bloodshot
    eyes?
Terror? No.
Despair? Perhaps.
What else?
Ah, poor ghosts—poor blind unseeing ghosts!
It is his self you see;
His self that does remember what he loved
    and what he wanted, and what he never had;

His self that can regret, that can reproach its
own self now; his self that gave itself, let
loose its hold of all but just itself.
Is that, then, nothing? Just his naked self,
pinning down a shaking world,
A single rivet driven down to hold a universe
together.

Go back, poor ghosts. Go back into your
graves.
He has no use for you, this nameless man.
Scholars, philosophers, men of God, leave
this man alone.
No lamp you lit will show his soul the way;
No name restore his lost identity.
The guns will chant his death march down the
world;
The flare of cannon light his dying;
The mute and nameless men beneath his feet
will welcome him beside them in the mud.
Take one last look and leave him standing
there,
Unfriended, unrewarded, and unknown.

Printed in England